349 DAYS

I WAS YOUNG, BUT I <u>WAS</u> A SOLDIER
A VIETNAM GRUNT'S STORY
By Slater Davis

Cover image of the author in the jungle by Dale Doege

DEDICATION

To Darrel and Larce

CONTENTS

ACKNOWLEDGMENTS

Let me begin by thanking a few folks. Top on the list is Becki, my wife and friend for over 46 years now. She has supported and encouraged me in my efforts to make sense out of the events from this time in our lives. Many thanks also go to the members of 4th Platoon of Bravo Company (Big Bad Bravo), 4th Battalion, 21st Infantry Regiment, 11th Light Infantry Brigade of the Americal Division, class of 1971, who taught me how to be a grunt (aka, an infantry soldier in Vietnam). I especially want to thank Vince Varel, Tim Frater, David Bruski, Tom Duran, and Dale Doege of 4th Platoon, and Charlie Dault of the CP Platoon and later Delta Company, 4th Battalion, 3rd Infantry Regiment, 198th Light Infantry Brigade, who read an early draft of this story and offered additional details and valuable suggestions. Thanks also go to Bruce Flaherty, a volunteer historian for Delta Company 4th/3rd, for the copies of daily action reports he provided to me from his research. And it was Laura Waltke, Becki's sister, who used her tendency toward detail and her skill as a proofreader to apply a lot of red ink to the pages, making this story much more readable and interesting.

Finally, I want to thank God for His hand in my life. I was not a Christian while I was in Vietnam (though I thought I was), coming to faith a few years after my return. Over time, however, I have come to see that God is intimately involved in the lives of men, and has sovereign care over the same. Some may disagree with that, or even scoff, and that is their privilege; but I will always be thankful for His protection over me before, during, and after Vietnam. For readers interested in my story of coming to faith, it can be found toward the end of this book.

All photographs are from my personal collection unless otherwise noted. All photographs are used with permission.

INTRODUCTION

During the past few years my sister, Helen, has gotten involved in family history and genealogy. We have had many conversations about this, and one thing that seems to frequently pop up is the phrase, "I wish I could have talked to so-and-so about that." That resonated with me and was part of the reason I started this writing project. The idea of doing something like this had been bouncing around in my head for quite some time and I finally decided, "Why not? Let's write it down." So, it began as an effort to tell my story to my family. I didn't want them sometime down the road to be saying, "I wish we had talked to Pop about that." Then it grew beyond that. Why? Who knows...maybe to give me something to do now that I'm retired, or maybe for some deeper reason I haven't YET figured out. I just know the urge is there.

A few years ago, as I began reuniting with some of my fellow grunts at reunions, I learned that my recollections about things and events, and what others remember about those same things and events, sometimes don't match. I don't think that means one version is right and the other is wrong. Rather, I believe that we each saw and experienced things from different physical and emotional positions. I also believe that memories of one event may get mixed in with memories of other events. I have also learned that my memory is not nearly as precise as it was back then. It has been 45 years since I was in Vietnam, you know. Additionally, some stories I have heard at reunions are not to be found in my memory at all. I have no explanation for that. I am told I was there. I am told I took part. In some cases I can see myself in a picture someone took, but when I search my memory it's not there. Go figure!

My tour in Vietnam was relatively easy compared to some. I once had a neighbor who served in the same area I served in, only three or four years earlier. He described it as WWII. I couldn't relate to his experience at all. Because of this, for years I felt as if I hadn't really done my part, at least as much as others had. My oldest son, Chuck, found it hard to believe that I could count on one hand the number of times I fired my M-16 during my tour. And, several years ago, I had a friend ask me, after he saw the movie "Platoon", if the movie depicted what Vietnam was really like. I had seen the movie and related to parts of it, but most of it was nothing like I experienced. This was in part due to the fact that the movie depicted a time in the Vietnam War before I was there. Things changed greatly in Vietnam between 1965 and 1971. I felt that some aspects of the movie were depicted accurately, at least from my perspective: arrival and departure of the soldier in Vietnam—alone, not as part of a larger unit; the pounding heartbeat of a soldier in night ambush as adrenaline rushes into the midst of the grip of fear; the nuisance of mosquitos at night—they were horrible; the suddenness of how things can happen beyond one's control; and, among other things, the youthfulness of the soldiers of Vietnam. I was 21 years old when I arrived in Vietnam, and I think I was one of the older ones in my units there. We only had one man over 30 in our unit, and he was a lifer (career soldier). The idea, however, that our squad leaders were warmongers or killing machines, and that our platoon leaders (lieutenants) were incompetent, as the movie depicted, was far from accurate, and I think a great disservice to all who have served. I never knew a "gung-ho, let's go get 'em" type of guy in my experience. I told my friend, "I could relate to some of it (the movie)." That was as far as I felt I needed to go, at the time. Now, it seems the time is different. And, as I have already said, "the urge is there" to write this down. Movies, books, The History Channel, and other media present many versions of what some experienced or viewed as reality in Vietnam, though the editor always had the final say; but, I have come to see that my experience cannot be compared to the experiences of others, or to perceptions or imaginations of others. My experience was shared with some wonderful men, and has a common thread with their experience; but my experience was mine, and mine alone. As you read through these pages, you will be exposed to things as I remember them; to the events and the feelings that went with them—the fears and the joys. I was young, but I <u>was</u> a soldier. I was a grunt in Vietnam. So, here goes...

BEGINNINGS

The year was 1969. I was married to my love, Becki, with son number one on the way; although at the time we didn't know he was a "he". We lived in Atlanta, Georgia, and I was employed by the local phone company as a residential installer in the Atlanta area, being hired in September. On December 1, 1969, the United States held their first draft lottery since 1942. The draft—selecting young men (ages 18 and up) for military service—had been the law of the land since just before WWII. During the Vietnam War there was much public dissent about the war, and the draft was one of the focal points of the dissenters. In part, because of all of the controversy surrounding the draft, the new draft lottery was created. (Later, the all-volunteer Army would completely replace the draft.) In the lottery, dates were drawn randomly. The order in which the dates were drawn was the order in which men eligible for the draft, based on their birthday, would be called into service. My birthday, July 13, was selected as number 42, which meant I would be called into service before someone born on July 11, which was drawn number 248, but after someone born on September 14, which was drawn number 1. Those eligible for the draft could be exempted from service for a number of reasons. From the day I first registered, at age 18, I had carried a 2-S deferment because I was attending college. However, in the fall of 1969 I dropped out of college and lost my student deferment because I wasn't able to figure out how to work full-time and go to college at night. I eventually figured this out later in life, but that's not part of this story. The thought of Vietnam hung over us on our first Christmas together—1969.

The year 1970 began with Vietnam staring me in the face. Early in the year I began inquiring about a fatherhood deferment. This was one of the many exemptions allowed and, since I had lost my student deferment, I was looking for another way to be excluded from service. I really didn't want to go into the Army—especially to Vietnam—and thought I could use our "expected arrival" as a way to avoid this. I met with my draft board and learned that fatherhood deferments were not available in my circumstance. I briefly considered packing up and moving to Canada. Many draft eligible men did this during those tumultuous years in America. Becki and I talked about it and decided it would not be a good idea. It really seemed cowardly to me. We both resigned ourselves to the reality that I would be drafted. It wasn't long into the new year that the process began. I received an official looking letter in the mail. The first line was all I needed to read: "You are hereby directed to present yourself for Armed Forces Physical Examination..." This was the first step—to see if I was physically able to serve in the military. My physical was to be done at the Military Induction Center on Ponce de Leon Avenue in Atlanta. It was less than five miles from where we lived. On the assigned day I was stuck, prodded, listened to, and given the complete work-over by military medical staff. I passed. With the physical completed, I knew it wouldn't be long before I received my "Greetings" letter from Uncle Sam. Sure enough, it came in the spring of that same year.

"Greetings: You are hereby ordered for induction into the Armed Forces of the United States…" That was a heart heavy moment. It was really happening. I had a date that I had to report, once again to the induction center in Atlanta; so we began the process of moving back home to Griffin, Georgia. Griffin was our hometown. My draft board was there, and it was also where Becki's mom lived. Becki planned to stay with her mom while I was in the Army. I had grown up in Griffin. It was a great place to be a kid; big enough to have some variety, but small enough to miss the 'big city' problems of the day. Folks knew their neighbors, and we slept with the windows open and the doors unlocked. I had been a paperboy for the Griffin Daily News from the seventh grade until I graduated from high school. Delivery was done by bicycle. I rode that bicycle all over Griffin, even when I wasn't delivering papers. I graduated from Griffin High School in 1967; met Becki in Griffin the following year at a friend's house; and had a couple of years of college under my belt when Becki and I got married in May, 1969. Everyone knew there was a war going on in Vietnam. It was on the news every night and in the paper every day. I had even attended a large gathering in 1966 in Atlanta, at Atlanta Stadium (then home of the Braves) while I was in high school. The event was called "Affirmation Vietnam" and was started by students at Emory University in Atlanta. It was a counter to the protests that were taking place against the war across America. The group wanted to let the troops serving in the war know they were supported. It had sounded like a good idea to me at the time. I remember a large group from Griffin driving to the event on a rainy day, joining thousands of others in our statement of support for the troops. My attendance at that rally was my only exposure to the Vietnam War, and all that revolved around it, until I would find myself right in the middle of it a few years later.

I left my job at the phone company, receiving a Military Leave of Absence—meaning they would hold my job for me, and got Becki settled in Griffin in time for me to report on my induction day. I remember the day I left Griffin to report to the induction center in Atlanta. Becki and her Mom drove me to the bus station. We all said our good-byes with hugs all around, hugging Becki with a long, melting into one another hug. I could feel her shudder as we embraced. I hated to let her go, but let her go I did; then I walked away and boarded the bus. As the bus began to pull away, I looked out of the bus window; I could see Becki crying really hard and her Mom trying to console her. That was really difficult... I didn't know what lay ahead for me, but now I realized, for the first time I guess, that what lay ahead for me actually lay ahead for both of us—I should say for the "three" of us, now that our first child was on the way. How this was to work out would only be learned with the passage of time.

TRAINEE

At the induction center in Atlanta I joined many others who were reporting at the same time to be sworn in. We were all gathered into a group and led in the speaking of our oath: "I, Slater Davis, do solemnly swear that I will support and defend the Constitution of the United States against all enemies, foreign and domestic; that I will bear true faith and allegiance to the same; and that I will obey the orders of the President of the United States and the orders of the officers appointed over me, according to regulations and the Uniform Code of Military Justice. So help me God." There...it was done. It was June 16, 1970. I now belonged to the U.S. Government, specifically, the U.S. Army. Late in the afternoon we all boarded a bus to Columbia, South Carolina, and the lovely environs of Fort Jackson.

I didn't know what to expect as the bus arrived at Fort Jackson in the middle of the night. As I stepped off that bus, I quickly learned that Drill Instructors (D.I.) were all they were built up to be in my imagination. There was a lot of yelling, screaming, and "in-your-face" intimidation. It was the middle of the night; we were formed into some kind of loose formation; and these guys were some kind of crazy! Screaming in our faces; running around the group. Singling-out men who didn't do exactly what they were told; we learned real quick that we were now nothing but lowly trainees. Welcome to the United States Army, trainee!! Then it was off to the company area that would become our home for the next eight weeks. This intimidation style of leadership continued well into Basic Training, though it seemed to ease up as time went by. I don't know if I got used to it, or the D.I.s were actually easing up.

One of the first things we had to do was get the traditional military haircut—talk about shearing the sheep—those barbers showed no mercy! I had gotten a haircut at home because my hair had some pretty good length to it; I also had some healthy sideburns and a big mustache. All of these were removed at home in hopes of making a good impression. Oh, the young can be so foolish! I arrived at Basic Training with nice, un-tanned skin where my hair, sideburns, and mustache had been. Talk about drawing attention to yourself. My 'white spots' got the attention of a D.I., and he made a spectacle of me in front of the other trainees, talking about my efforts to avoid being noticed!

We were also issued all of the gear we would need as newly arrived trainees in the United States Army: fatigues, khakis, dress uniforms, hats, underwear, dress shoes, boots, blankets, pillows-all of it. The Army issued each of us two pairs of boots. They were the standard black Army boots. We learned how to keep them properly polished in what was known as a spit shine. Some guys got really good at that and could make their boots almost reflective. We had to paint a white dot on the back, at the top, of one pair. This gave the D.I. a quick way to make sure we were alternating our boots every day. One day was paint day; the next was no-paint day. This did two things.

It got both pairs of boots broken in good; and it kept us from setting aside one pair to always be ready for inspection.

Somewhere along the way during the first few days in the Army I remember receiving a gift packet from the Red Cross and another from the Gideons. The Red Cross pack included a notebook and pen, along with some other toiletry items. The Gideons provided me with a pocket-sized Bible that contained the Psalms, Proverbs, and New Testament. After Basic Training, that little Bible stayed in my shirt pocket all the way through Vietnam….

Every morning we would be awakened by the yelling and screaming of the D.I. Those guys just loved to make a lot of noise early in the morning. Sometimes they would bang on the wall or the ends of the bunks. The idea was: you trainees better get up and moving…right now! We had just a few minutes to get up, make our bed, shave, shower, get dressed, and fall outside into formation. At each morning formation, the D.I. would walk his way through our ranks taking a really close look at each of us. Early in basic training, one of the new recruits in our platoon was called out of the formation to stand in front of the entire platoon. He was then ordered to dry shave in front of our formation because he hadn't done a very good job shaving that morning. As he was doing this, and while we were trying not to look, the D.I. moved down the line examining all of his trainees. He took a close look at me and a few others with heavy beard growth; I remember he again noted my "white spots"; and then he let us all know we would be the next ones to dry shave in public if we didn't take up the habit of shaving twice a day. I had no problem whatsoever with shaving twice a day after that!

After first formation every morning we would go off on a run. The first few days of this were pure torture. I was a morning person; breakfast was the first thing I did every day at home. Running on an empty stomach was not for me; but it was the Army way, and I belonged to them now. The first couple of days I got really nauseated and clammy sweaty on those early morning runs, but there was no way I was going to fall out and be subject to a D.I.'s wrath. I stuck with it and, by the third day, I was doing okay. After the run we would file into the mess hall for breakfast. This was like no breakfast I had ever had. I was used to eggs and toast or French toast, or pancakes, maybe cereal and a banana. But that wasn't the Army way here. We had some kind of slop on toast. Yuk! What's a guy to do? I was hungry, so I ate it—all of it; and I got used to it.

The Army had a certain way for doing everything. Part of Basic Training was learning this important truth. If this principle could be learned, it made life a lot easier in the details. Thus, we learned how to keep our barracks straight and clean, the Army way. Our bunks had to be made a certain way. No deviation was allowed, and no wrinkles in the blanket were allowed. We each had a wall locker and foot locker. And both lockers had to be organized the Army way; everything in its place. Every bunk was identical. Every locker was identical. All foot lockers and bunks were perfectly aligned on either side of the wide open sleeping quarters, with all traffic going down the middle of the length of the building; to and from exit doors at each end. The floors were what seemed to be one continuous sheet of green linoleum stretching from one side of the building to the other and the full length of the building. This too had to be kept shiny clean. This was done using mops and a big floor buffer. It took some effort to master the buffer. Our D.I. gathered us around and showed us how it worked. The trick was to allow the buffer to "float" by holding it just right. This technique made it easy to control. Several guys, including me, were called up to give the buffer a try. My first attempt at using the buffer drew much attention from my fellow trainees and a bit of ridicule from the D.I. I grabbed the handle and turned the buffer on. The buffer took complete control of the situation, crashing into foot lockers and beds before I could turn it off. I dragged it back to the center aisle, and tried again. Soon I had it mastered and was buffing away.

Having everything in its place was not enough. There was no dirt or dust allowed anywhere. A white-glove inspection was a trainee's nightmare. The inspector, D.I. or officer, would wear a white glove and wipe his finger tips on everything. There had better not be any dust on that glove when he finished! We were in old, two-story, WWII-era barracks that let in a lot of outside air. This meant there was a lot of dust in our barracks. We returned from a run once and while we were gone our barracks had been inspected by one of the officers of the company. What we found when we entered the barracks really made everyone mad. Lockers were opened, foot lockers

14

were turned over, and beds had their linens and blankets removed, all piled on the floor. The place was a disaster. Something had been out of place. It only took one man missing a step and the whole platoon suffered. We were given a set time to put everything in order and prepare for another inspection. When the time was up we were called out to formation, and the building was inspected again. We passed. This happened several times...learning to do things the Army way.

It seemed we ran everywhere we went, always in formation and always shouting out those crazy cadence calls echoing our D.I. who ran with us. Here is an example of one cadence I remember. The D.I. would shout each line and we would repeat it:

"I want to be an Airborne Ranger....
I want to go to Vietnam....
I want to be an Airborne Ranger...
I want to kill some Viet Cong...
1,2...3,4...1,2...3,4..."

Over and over we would chant, and on and on we would run. The cadence would help us keep pace and stay in step as we learned to move as a group. Even today when I go for a walk I sometimes find a cadence running through my head helping me keep a steady pace. But today the cadences follow a different tune.

And boy did we do calisthenics! I never played sports in school, so this was all new to me. Sit-ups; push-ups; jumping jacks; chin-ups; the list seemed never ending. One of the most tortuous exercises was lying flat on our backs and raising our legs. With our hands clasped together behind our heads, while lying flat on our backs, we would raise our legs about six or eight inches off the ground, keeping our knees locked and legs straight. Then, on command of the D.I., we would spread our legs and hold them in place. Then, again on command, we would bring them back together, still holding them off the ground. One D.I. would be shouting the commands to this company of trainees while others walked through the formation yelling at individuals who were groaning or dropping their legs to the ground. Gradually the legs would begin to bend to relieve the pain in the abdomen. This brought more shouts from the D.I.s walking through the formation. Eventually, when the command was given to drop our legs, there was a collective "ugh" announced by the entire company. If the lead D.I. didn't like this, we would do it all over again.

The D.I.s seemed to enjoy the torture they put us through. Some were better at it than others. And a few of them seemed a bit more laid back. But I never saw any of them show pity to any of us poor trainees, the recipients of their 'torture'! Their job was to get us into shape, both physically and mentally. And they knew their stuff. As a trainee, it was best to get your stuff done and not stand out, or draw attention to yourself. Some of the guys in the company just couldn't cut it, for whatever reason. These poor guys got a lot of focused attention from the D.I.s. I really felt for them. They were pushed extra hard. They were intimidated and yelled at more than the rest of us. For those who couldn't make the grade there was a special company they would be transferred to in an attempt to improve their physical abilities. That company must have been absolute torture. If a guy couldn't make it at that level, I think he was discharged from the Army.

We had one guy in our platoon who had difficulty with the physical training and with all the other stuff we were being trained to do. He couldn't keep his bunk straight, his locker neat, or even wear his uniform properly. He was a real 'misfit'. At every inspection (and there were many of them), it seemed he would do something wrong that affected the entire platoon. This would result in extra running or calisthenics, or a trashed barracks for all of us. One night, in the middle of the night, I heard a loud commotion upstairs in our barracks. I had no idea what was going on, but I found out the next morning at formation. We were lining up for our morning formation and run, and here comes our 'misfit'. He was all bruised up. One of his eyes was swollen, and his face was all red and bruised. He looked pretty bad. He had been given a blanket party, which was the commotion I had heard during the night. A blanket party happened when a group of guys throw a blanket over another man while he is sleeping. While he is covered, unable to see who is attacking him, he is pummeled by his attackers. I guess the goal of this activity was to get the victim's attention and improve his behavior. Within just a few days of this incident, our company's 'misfit' was no longer with us. I never knew what happened to him. The attackers were never identified, and nothing was ever said about the incident.

In addition to the running and physical conditioning, we heard a lot of lectures on different topics. Some of these topics were: military ranks and who to salute; proper wearing of the uniform; the Geneva Convention; rules of war; and the different weapons we were trained on. Classrooms or lectures always went with any field training we received.

RIFLES, GAS, AND SHOTS

After one morning run, I remember the entire company was brought back into the company area and ordered to move between two of our WWII-era barracks. There was a podium against one of the barrack buildings, and soon our Company Commander arrived at the podium. We all jumped to attention, and he told us to take a seat. As one, the entire company did just that, on the ground between the buildings. He told us he was going to introduce us to the M-16 Rifle. He talked a little about it; then, to everyone's surprise, he pulled one out from inside the podium and leveled it at us. With the rifle set on full automatic, he emptied a full magazine of blanks, scaring the hell out of every one of us. The D.I.s loved it. The commander had our undivided attention and then proceeded to tell us all about the M-16. In the days that followed, we were all issued our very own M-16. We learned to disassemble and reassemble it, how to care for it, and then how to shoot it.

We took many trips to the rifle range to become proficient on the M-16. The entire company would form up and run to a staging location to be loaded into the backs of big trucks. We were all warned about the dangers of exiting these trucks by grabbing the frame and jumping off, though this is how we disembarked at every stop. Apparently the danger was from wearing a ring, and snagging the ring on the frame of the truck as one jumped out. This could easily remove a finger from the jumper's hand. There were pictures at various places in the company area, and at the ranges, of a severed finger wearing a ring. We were encouraged to remove our rings whenever we rode in the trucks. I decided I would be careful—my wedding ring was staying right where it belonged.

At the rifle range the entire company would line up in a single line along the firing line and each trainee would take a position. Everyone had ear plugs, and it was mandatory that they be worn. The D.I.s were spaced behind the firing line. Their job was to be sure everyone followed the directions of the rifle range instructor. Once everyone was in place, we were issued live ammunition; then we all prepared to begin shooting. The instructor would call out, "Ready on the left! Ready on the right! Ready on the firing line! Commence firing!" That's when we could begin shooting. When we finished shooting, all weapons would be cleared and we would step back from our firing positions. We were told to be sure that we had no ammo or spent cartridges on our person. Then we would march off the range in single file. As we passed the range instructor we would each declare, "No brass or ammo, sergeant!"

On our first trip to the range we were seated on a set of bleachers. It was the same as all instruction in Basic Training. The range instructor would arrive; we would all jump up to attention. Then he would shout, "Good morning men!" and we would reply, "Good morning sergeant (or whatever his rank was)!" Then we would be seated for the instructor to begin. At the range, the range instructor told us the rules to be followed at all times while at the range. The Army was pretty particular about some things; the rifle range was one of them. It was all about safety! Once the orientation was complete, the remainder of our first time at the range was spent zeroing our weapons. This meant we were adjusting the sights on the rifle to fit our personal posture and aiming view. We shot at targets that were pretty close to us. After a few shots the targets were inspected to see how close we came to what we were aiming at. The M-16 front site could be manipulated to adjust the line of fire, either up or down, depending on where the rounds hit. Once we had the sights aligned properly, we then began working on shooting a tight shot group. The goal was to get a grouping of three shots into a very small area on the target. It took several trips to the range for me to get the feel of the M-16 and master the tight shot group.

Once the basics of shooting the M-16 were mastered, we moved on to the silhouette ranges. The silhouette ranges really tested our abilities on the M-16. They were fun. We shot at metal silhouettes of the human torso that would pop up at varying ranges in front of each firing position. The distances ranged from 50 meters to 300 meters. If the silhouette was hit, it would fall over. I knew immediately if I was on target. Of course, if I missed, I had to figure out which way to adjust my aim. I could pop a 50-meter target without aiming; the 300-meter targets took a little practice; but with practice, I got the hang of it. We were eventually graded on our proficiency. I scored as an expert, which meant I hit 36 out of the 40 targets in the allotted time.

Another memory I have from basic training was being selected for Fireman duty. When my name was called and I was told I was going to some special training, I had a glimmer of hope this might be the break that would keep me from going to Vietnam. I soon learned that being a Fireman in our old barracks meant that I was one of those responsible for 'firing' the gas water heaters early in the morning, so when everyone else got up they could have hot showers. That's the Army for you!

Gas mask training is something I think all veterans remember from basic training. I sure do! We were all given gas masks and told how to put them on properly. Then we were tested to see how fast we could put them on. The instructor would check us out to be sure we had gotten it done quickly and correctly. The training on the masks was not complete without the 'gas room'. This was a building that a few guys would enter together. There was an instructor in the building wearing his gas mask. Once we were all inside and ready, the instructor released some gas and shouted, "Gas, Gas, Gas!" I'm not sure what it was, but I think it was a version of tear gas. Then we all removed our masks from their cases and put them on, clearing them as fast as we could, so we could breathe. After listening to the instructor for a bit, while wearing our masks, with the gas all around, we were ordered to remove our masks and yell out our name, rank, and serial number. If we were successful in one breath, we were then ordered to do more stuff. The instructor wanted us to breathe. We all had to wait until everyone in our group had taken at least one good breath.

Pity the guy who breathed first; he had to wait for the rest of us while he continued to enjoy the gas. I never figured out how this particular approach to training was helpful. I just remember my eyes, nose, and throat burning like crazy. Then we were all shown the exit and rushed outside. We were coughing like crazy, moaning and groaning, and all the while our eyes and noses were running. The Army didn't even provide us with tissues!

Then there were the shots. Yes sir, we all had to have shots— lots of shots! Over the years, I guess the Army had figured out the most efficient way to deliver shots to a bunch of trainees. We had been on a morning run and, instead of returning to our company area, we turned into a field that had a group of guys dressed in white lined up on one side of the field. We were brought to a stop and told to remove our shirts. Then, by platoon and squad, we formed a line and walked through this double line of guys in white. These were medics, or medical folks, and they were loaded up with air-powered syringes. We were told to step up between the first set of guys and be real still. When it was my turn, I stepped between the two guys. Then each of them grabbed one of my arms and 'shot' me with their air-powered syringe. This happened on multiple occasions, sometimes getting more than two shots per stop. One of our guys didn't like getting shots, and he jerked his arm right while the medic was applying the air-powered syringe. Well, the patient got a nice little rip in his arm from the air pressure. There was never anyone else who moved at all after that for the rest of the shots we received!

Toward the end of Basic Training, after we had learned all of our close order drill and marching techniques, we were tested on what we had learned. There were several booths set up in an outside pavilion with an instructor in each booth. One at a time, all of the trainees were called to a booth where the instructor began to bark out drill orders: "attention," "at ease," "attention," "left face," "about face," "right face," "present arms", and on and on. I was doing really great until I got distracted by the instructor in the next booth. My instructor barked one thing, and the instructor next door barked something different. I did exactly what the instructor next door said. This really made my instructor mad, and he had a few choice comments for me and the quality of my responses. I felt like an idiot, but I passed anyway.

Also near the end of basic training, we went on a long march and spent three days and two nights in the field sleeping in tents. During the day we would do training exercises and other stuff, all while wearing full gear and carrying an M-16. On the last day we closed out the bivouac area, put on our gear and headed back to the company area. At this point I was assigned the role of carrying the company flag, which meant I was out in front of the company with the head D.I. It was an eight-mile march, some of which was a run instead of a march. Toward the end of the trip we took a detour through the 'sand pit.' Anyone familiar with Fort Jackson back then knew what the sand pit was. It was a pretty long area that had been filled with many truckloads of nice, soft white sand, piled up in a long line forming a small ridge. Around the edges of the pile of sand was more, nice, soft white sand. Imagine walking on the beach behind where the surf packs the sand; this would come close to describing the difficulty of walking in the sand pit. But we weren't walking; we were running. And we were running with all our gear on. The company did several laps around the pit at a slower and slower jog. I thought I was going to fall out. I guess the head D.I. saw I was wavering and he began to 'encourage' me to keep on with some 'very choice' words of motivation. I kept pushing and made it back to the company area. Needless to say, when we arrived back at the company area, we were all exhausted.

After many miles of marching, running, crawling, and being treated like an animal in a herd, basic training was almost over. All that lay ahead was being assigned a Military Occupational Specialty (MOS), orders for our next duty station, and graduation. Though I had scored well on the battery of tests I took when I first arrived, I was given the MOS of 11B (Infantry). That might have had something to do with the answer I gave at every inquiry about selecting a specific 'career path.' I always asked, "Will it keep me out of Vietnam?" The closest I ever came to getting a yes answer to that question was regarding joining the EOD team. When I learned that EOD stood for explosive ordinance disposal (the bomb squad), I figured I would be better off in Vietnam. No other career paths could ever guarantee I would miss Vietnam, so I never signed up. Anyway, who ever heard of a 'career path' for a draftee who didn't want to be there—and had a good job with the phone company waiting for him? Was that my first real exposure to Military Intelligence? Maybe so!

ADVANCED INFANTRY TRAINING

I didn't have to travel far to reach my next duty station. Advanced Infantry Training (A.I.T.) was held right there at Fort Jackson. During the next eight weeks I became pals with three other guys, and we did a lot together. There was Jerry, Bruce and Causey. I've lost contact with Jerry and Causey, but got back in touch with Bruce a few years ago. Bruce had gone on to Ranger training after A.I.T.; then I saw him several months later in Vietnam as part of the 75th Rangers, after I had been there for a while.

Some weekends during A.I.T. we would get a weekend pass. A couple of times I actually flew home to be with Becki, but most weekends we would just go into Columbia to get off the base. Nobody wanted to be hanging around on the base all weekend, not that there was a lot to do in Columbia; but at least there wasn't a duty officer downtown to look you up and give you something to do. Who wants to have their Saturday interrupted with a call to "police the area"? Policing the area meant everyone would be lined up and walk across an area, picking up anything that didn't belong there—even cigarette butts. The Army had trained us in the proper way of disposing a cigarette. When we finished our smoke, we were to twist the end of the spent cigarette between our fingers until all remaining tobacco fell out onto the ground. Then the cigarette butt was to be put in our pockets, to be disposed of in the next trash receptacle we passed. The Army knew how to keep their place clean—that was for sure. The activity of training kept us busy, but in the down times there were always thoughts of home. These were lonely times. There were the phone calls and letters, but the touch, the caresses, and the togetherness were missing. It was good to be kept busy in training.

A.I.T. was preparing us for our military specialty. Everyone in the Army had a specialty, and ours was The Infantry! Upon graduation, we would be able to wear the blue rope over the right shoulder of our dress uniform, signifying to everyone what our specialty was—The Infantry. We qualified on and/or fired a number of weapons including the M-14 and M-16 rifles, 45 caliber pistol, the M-79 grenade launcher, the M-60 machine gun, and the 50-caliber machine gun. We also learned the proper technique to use when throwing a hand grenade and how to fire the L.A.W. (Light Anti-Tank Weapon). We learned battle tactics and small group maneuver during conflict. One training exercise we did had the goal of teaching us to be able to fire our weapon quickly, without taking precise aim. For this exercise, we were issued BB guns. We all wore our shirt sleeves down and were issued wire-screen masks to cover our faces. We were divided into groups; one group would lie in ambush while the other group would walk a trail through the ambush site. Then we reversed roles. The ambushers would open fire on the guys on the trail, and the guys on the trail would see how quickly they could respond with their BB guns. Of course, the guys in the ambush team had a distinct advantage. I learned that a BB can carry a nice little punch, even thru a fatigue shirt sleeve.

In A.I.T. we also learned how to use a compass and read a map. After receiving instruction in the techniques required to do these, we were transported to the compass navigation course. We were divided into small groups and had to navigate, using a compass and map—from a starting point, to a mid-point, then to a third point, and then back to the starting point. We were given the compass direction and distance to each point from the previous point, and given a map that showed the terrain and landmarks. We shot an azimuth (a compass direction) from our starting point and off we went. If we got lost or disoriented, we could quickly find out where we were if we could spot two landmarks. All we needed to do was shoot an azimuth to each landmark from our location, spot them on the map, and draw a line at the same degrees of our azimuth. Wherever the lines crossed was our location. Our little group made it through this exercise without any hitches and in a good time. This was a great learning exercise.

We also went on night maneuvers. As I remember it, though our days were full, we did a lot more night work in A.I.T. than we did in Basic Training. Toward the end of A.I.T., we spent several days in the field on bivouac. We had full gear on the entire time, even our weapons—which were loaded with blanks. We did a lot of patrolling and setting out ambushes from a perimeter where we built bunkers and filled sandbags. The bunkers had to be dug out and covered with logs (provided by the Army) and then covered with sandbags. We would actually get in firefights, shooting blanks, with other groups during our patrols and ambushes. This gave us a greater sense of reality as we prepared for war. One of the mornings we awoke to a thick frost covering everything. Here we were preparing for Vietnam and everyone was wearing jackets and gloves. Shaving that morning was quite an experience!

On one occasion we had to escape from a 'POW camp' in the middle of the night and find our way back to a home base camp. For the POW camp escape, we were all sitting in little groups in a fenced compound with guards in watch towers. Suddenly, simulated gunfire broke out, along with a few explosions. The gates were thrown open and the instructors yelled, "Go! Go! Go, get out of here!" Off we went in all sorts of directions. We had been told the 'enemy' would be pursuing us and, if caught, we would be brought back to the POW camp and held until the exercise was over. We were also told not to walk along any roads to find our way back to our base area; but that seemed to be a counterproductive order, so our little group decided to make it straight to the nearest road and keep a sharp eye for headlights. It worked. We made it back to base in short order, only having to dive into the ditch a few times when vehicles came along. I took all of these activities in stride, tried to learn everything I could, and had some fun with them at the same time.

On another long night in A.I.T., I learned that I could sleep with my eyes open. We had been at it all day and late into the night. When we finally made it back to our barracks, we were exhausted. Everyone wanted a shower and then some sleep. For me, it was my night for first shift on 'hall duty'. The barracks we had in A.I.T. were much more modern than the WWII-era barracks we lived in during Basic Training. It was more like a college dorm building than a barracks. There were two sets of bunk beds in each room that entered into a long hallway down the middle of the building. Hall duty consisted of sitting in a classroom-style desk at the end of the hall, monitoring traffic in the building. While everyone headed for the showers, I headed for the desk at the end of the hall. I got comfortable sitting at the desk, just staring down the hall. A little later, one of our sergeants came up to me (I was later told it happened this way...) and began speaking to me. When I didn't respond, he waved his hand in front of my face. Still, I didn't respond. I finally 'woke up' when he shook me. He was not very happy with me, but was also confused. I was sitting perfectly erect at the desk, eyes wide open, staring down the hall; apparently, however, I was sound asleep. Well, I finished my round of 'hall duty' that night in the standing position beside the desk. My shower and bunk that night sure did feel good when my duty was complete.

It wasn't long before A.I.T. was approaching an end, and the anxiety level began to rise among the troops wondering about orders and destinations. Some would go to Germany, some to Korea. Most would go to Vietnam. I got my orders...Vietnam. I wondered what lay ahead for me. I received a few weeks' leave before having to report to Fort Lewis Washington, the staging location for troops going to Vietnam. Graduation day from A.I.T. was October 23, 1970. I flew home to Orange Park, Florida, where Becki's mom had recently moved. I was met at the Jacksonville airport by Becki's brother, Charlie. He told me that Becki was in the hospital and had delivered twin girls. It was a long drive from the airport to the hospital. Charlie spent this time filling my head with all sorts of ideas about what it was going to be like having twin daughters. When I got to the hospital, I learned that Charlie had been razing me the entire drive! Becki was actually still in labor. Our first son, Charles Edward (Chuck) was born in the early morning hours of October 24, at the Naval Air Station Hospital in Jacksonville. He was two weeks old when I left to spend a few days in Atlanta with my family before reporting to Fort Lewis, in Washington State, for deployment to Vietnam.

Saying goodbye to Chuck at the Jacksonville airport, on my way to Atlanta and then Vietnam, November 1970.

I hoped I would be home to celebrate his first birthday; but first there was this 'long tunnel' I had to walk through—and I couldn't see the other end of it....

I spent a day or two at Fort Lewis before a group of us were gathered together for shipment to Vietnam. I did not know anyone on the flight over, just guys I had met in the short time I had been at Fort Lewis. I felt all alone...in my tunnel...and couldn't see the other end.

VIETNAM

We flew over to Vietnam on Flying Tiger Airlines, a commercial airliner contracted to the military. We flew through Alaska, and its snow-lined runways, to allow a change in crew on the airplane, and then on to Japan. We had a short layover in Japan, and some of the guys on board went inside the building. I just stayed on the plane. We got a different group of stewardesses, our third group; I noticed that each group had gotten progressively older and uglier. Was this another one of the Army's ways to prepare us for what lay ahead? Or, maybe, the pay scale was different for each leg of the journey, and they got to choose based on their seniority. Who knows what was behind it? The change was obvious. We left Japan; our next stop was Cam Ranh Bay, South Vietnam. I remember the pilot telling us, as we approached Vietnam, the temperature in the airplane would be adjusted to help us acclimate to the heat of South Vietnam. It got pretty hot in that airplane, but when they opened the door and I disembarked, I thought I had stepped into an oven. It was November 22, 1970. It was hot and it stunk. The tarmac was a busy place. The one thing I noticed was that no one was carrying a weapon. Wasn't this Vietnam? Were these guys crazy? What was going on here?

I was soon boarding a C-130 cargo plane to be flown up to Chu Lai (pronounced choo lie), a couple of hundred miles to the north. Chu Lai was the home of the 23rd Infantry Division (Americal Division), and I spent several days there going through in-country orientation at the Combat Training Center. The instructors were the real deal, from the bush (the field). They didn't hold back in their descriptions of what lay ahead for us in the Infantry. They discussed the Division's area of operations (AO), map reading, survival tactics, dealing with the local population and, among other things, tactics used by the Viet Cong (VC). I also learned here that I was a newbie and I better watch and learn from the guys who had been here a while. Ok, great! I had graduated from trainee to newbie! Was this progress?

At night in Chu Lai, at the Combat Training Center, I pulled bunker security along the South China Sea. I was anxious about this. This was Vietnam. It's on the news. People were getting killed over here! Why was everyone around me so relaxed? In reality, there really wasn't a need to be anxious because Chu Lai was a relatively safe area at this time. The bunker security was probably more for me than for the base security. I remember my first night in Chu Lai. After pulling bunker duty, I walked into this large hut full of beds where we were to sleep. There must have been 40 or more beds, half on each side of a center aisle. Way down at the other end of the building was one guy, stretched out, sound asleep. He was the only other person in the room; but there was a critter in there. Sitting happily on this guy's chest was one very large rat. The guy was totally oblivious. When the rat saw me, he scurried away. I thought, 'I'm going to sleep in here?' Well, I did. And, as far as I know, I never got a visit from a rat; but then, who knows—I was sleeping.

Chu Lai had not received any incoming rocket or mortar fire in over six months, but while I was in Chu Lai the VC decided it was time to drop a few in. I was in the mess hall eating supper when they hit. The rockets didn't hit close to us, but we heard them. The guys that had been there a while didn't even look up. But this newbie and others around me all began looking around, wondering what we should do next. After the first two explosions, the base sirens began screaming. This newbie wasn't going to sit there one more minute. I grabbed my cup of ice cream and dashed out of the mess hall as fast as my young legs could move, running to the nearest shelter. Once in the shelter, I caught my breath and then finished my ice cream. The attack was over about as soon as it started. The "all clear" was sounded and things settled down, but the base stayed on "yellow alert" until the next morning. That meant more guys in the bunkers and more guys awake at the same time. Bunker security was a little more serious on this night. The next morning, the sun came up, just like it had before, and all was well.

It was in Chu Lai, at the Combat Training Center (CTC), that I was introduced to one of the most unpleasant experiences I ever had. Several of us newbies were selected to "burn shit". I don't know what else to call it. That's what we did. The latrine was a plywood structure with screened sections in the sides to allow the breeze to blow through—a really good idea. The interior on one side was built up for sitting and taking care of business. Each latrine had several 'positions' for participants to use while answering nature's call. These positions were just holes cut in the plywood decking, and a toilet seat was nailed down on top of the hole. Below each of these positions was half of a 55-gallon drum. Each half-drum was 'strategically' placed under its position to catch human waste. The job of keeping everyone healthy required disposing of the human waste. The process fell to the newbies. We had to drag the drums out from under the latrine a safe distance. Then we poured kerosene into the drums and lit the kerosene on fire. While the fire was burning, the contents had to be stirred to ensure that everything was completely burned up. What a stench! Where are the showers?!? Oh yeah, let's not forget the "pee-tubes". If all you had to do was pee, you didn't have

Tom Duran (TD) enjoying the "pause" at a 'pee tube'.

to go all the way to the latrine. Scattered all over the area were "pee-tubes". These were 55-gallon drums (or some other cylindrical shaped object) that were buried in the sand and surrounded on three sides with a flimsy visual barrier about four feet high for privacy. The top of the drum was covered with wire screen; the drum itself was filled with sand; and I suspect it had the bottom cut out. Just step outside and enjoy the 'pause that refreshes'! Welcome to Vietnam!

After enduring several days at the CTC, I learned that I would be assigned to a unit about 50 miles south of Chu Lai. Soon I joined Bravo Company, 4th Battalion, 21st Infantry Regiment of the 11th Light Infantry Brigade near Duc Pho (pronounced duck fo), South Vietnam, at Fire Support Base (FSB) Bronco. Duc Pho was a small village in the Quang Ngai (pronounced quang ni) province—this province being located at the southern end of I Corps. (South Vietnam was divided into U.S. Military regions called Corps.) I Corps was the northernmost portion, with its northern edge bordering on North Vietnam at the demilitarized zone (DMZ). Bronco was the headquarters for the 11th LIB, known as The Jungle Warriors. I was assigned to 4th Platoon in Bravo Company. This platoon was traditionally a weapons platoon that carried a mortar and mortar rounds on missions in the field in order to support the rest of the company in the event of enemy contact. Just before my arrival, the platoon had been converted to a regular rifle platoon. When I joined the platoon, it was split about half-and-half 11-B guys (infantry) and 11-C guys (mortar men). One of the first things I learned after arriving at BBB (Big Bad Bravo) headquarters and being assigned to the 4th Platoon, was what to take in my rucksack (back pack) and what to leave behind. Having dry socks and a dry T-shirt were top on the list. A towel was good, so were a sleeping shirt and a set of bush booties. (The sleeping shirt was a warm pullover long-sleeved shirt, and the booties were a very comfortable slip-on moccasin style shoe that I wore sometimes at night.) An entrenching tool was a must. Grab an ammo can for personal things (paper, pen, etc.) and a plastic bag for my instamatic camera. Then there was the poncho liner, air mattress (maybe), one pound of C-4 (plastic explosive), bug juice (liquid insect repellant), three or four frags (hand grenades), a couple of smoke grenades, machete, M-16 ammo, M-60 machine gun ammo, at least one claymore and clacker. (The claymore was an anti-personnel mine and the clacker was the device used to detonate it. The claymore was full of small, metal balls that would be shot forward in a spreading pattern when the mine was detonated.) Also important were one or two trip flares, more ammo, and water—lots of water—and C-rations. I had to carry three days' worth of supplies for myself, and everyone carried ammo for the M-60 guy. The total weight of my rucksack was well above 50 pounds, especially at the beginning of a mission. I was also told to leave all underwear behind. Yep! Even with boxers, not briefs, the heat was impossible. Jock itch and rash were not worth the effort of wearing shorts. And my dog tags had to be removed from the chain around my neck and one laced into each of my boot strings. There were two reasons for this. First, the dog tags could click together and make a little noise at the most inopportune time; second, having a dog tag laced into each boot would make it easier to be identified if I hit a booby trap and got separated from my feet. Welcome to the realities of Vietnam (aka The 'Nam). I was placed on the first resupply bird to the field so I could officially join my platoon. Ok, here I was… now it begins. My head was full of questions. How long will I be a newbie? What will the bush be like? Will I know what to do? Will I make it? I stepped off the chopper into the rice paddies of South Vietnam and joined 4th Platoon, not knowing what would happen next, and not knowing another person in the entire company. I was alone…in my tunnel…and still couldn't see the other end.

THE RICE BOWL

I'll never forget my first night in the bush. I stepped off the resupply chopper and joined my new platoon in the Rice Bowl west of Duc Pho. This area, I learned later, was pacified and our primary mission was to keep the VC from encroaching in the area. As I stepped off that chopper I had no idea what the Rice Bowl was like. All I knew was that I was in Vietnam—the place where, according to the news back home and the staff at the CTC, there were enemy running around killing grunts every day.

A picture of the Rice Bowl, looking northwest from LZ Debbie.

The Rice Bowl was appropriately named, for there were rice paddies everywhere; around the edges of this valley was a ring of mountains, except where the valley met the South China Sea, giving the appearance of a large bowl. It was really a beautiful place, full of green shaded shapes that were the rice paddies, as seen from the air. The rice paddies were full of water during the growing season and separated by berms that the Vietnamese who cultivated them walked on. I learned that GIs walked on them too. Scattered in the area were small hamlets, each with several hooches that the Vietnamese lived in; around the hooches one could find other items growing, some cultivated, some not, like bamboo.

I thought I was seeing VC behind every blade of grass, and I had only been off the chopper two minutes! As I looked around at my new platoon mates, I noticed everyone was relaxed and calm. I was thinking, "What's wrong with these guys? Don't they know the VC are everywhere?" I was taken over to meet LT (short for lieutenant) in the platoon perimeter. LT Vince Varel was our platoon leader. I remember Vince as being a quiet guy, but very capable. I never really got to know Vince until after 'Nam, but he led us safely during his time as platoon leader. He introduced me to a couple of guys and assigned me to a squad leader, Tim Frater. The platoon had set up its perimeter in an area around a burned-out hooch. The area was elevated a bit higher than the rice paddies around it, so it gave good visibility for a long way, except for one corner of the perimeter. There was one corner of this place that was adjacent to an area completely grown over with thick bamboo, the big stuff. It was really tall, really big around, and really dense. I was told this would be my position for the night. Hmmm...I am stationed eight or ten feet from this stand of bamboo that completely blocks my view of anything beyond it; and between me and the bamboo is one of those well-traveled berms. There were guys on either side of me, and we would share the duty of keeping our area secure during the night. I looked around at the rest of the area, and every other position could see over a hundred yards without obstruction—but not me. I could only see ten feet. I didn't like it. I don't know if the assignment was a way to keep me safe on my first night, but as the night would prove, it was scary to me.

I began to meet some of the guys in the squad and platoon and was starting to settle in a bit. Night time was settling in, too, and I quickly learned that you better get whatever you want to get done before it gets dark. After dark, no one does anything...no light, no conversation above a whisper, no unnecessary movement—just quiet, listening, and sleeping. I was assigned a time slot for "watch" and told to go ahead and get some sleep. Yeah, right! Sleep? Who are you kidding? My first night in the bush and I was not very sleepy just yet! I did nod off, however, after a bit of quietness and, before long, I was being nudged to wake up for my turn at security. I knew how long I had and then I would wake up the next guy. I sat up, got my bearings in the total darkness, and listened to the other guy get comfortable in his spot on the ground as he dozed off. Then I listened. It was really quiet, eerily quiet; and it was dark, really dark. The bamboo in front of me made it even darker than it was. Then I heard something. What was that? Then silence! The only thing I could hear was the pounding of my heart in my ears. I'm really wired up...but all is quiet. Then I heard it again. I am so tense! I'm not sure what to do. Do I wake up one of the guys? Do I blast at the noise

An example of a hooch in the Rice Bowl.

with my M-16? Then it's quiet again...well, except for my heart beating louder than before. The longer I sit, the louder my heart beats. It's like my body is firing on all cylinders above the tach redline. I'm sweating. Am I hot, or am I scared to death? Maybe a little of both! Is a VC trying to slip through the bamboo in front of me? If so, would I see him before he sees me? A little breeze blows through and cools my sweating head...I hear the noise again. That's when my brain clicks into gear...breeze, noise, no breeze, no noise. Yep, after a few more minutes I had it figured out. It was the stalks of bamboo clicking against each other every time the breeze blew by. Whew! I began to relax just a little bit and, before long, I couldn't hear my heart beating anymore and it was time to wake up the next guy for security. I crawled over and nudged the guy next to me, got him awake, and then I lay down on the ground and listened to the bamboo click as I finally drifted off to sleep. Then the sun came up. I had made it. My first night in the bush was behind me. Maybe I can do this after all....

It wasn't long before I began getting to know the guys and learning the daily routine. I learned how to use C-4 to cook with (C-4 was a plastic explosive; it came in one-pound blocks. To cook with it, I would break off a small piece, place it on the ground where I was going to cook, and hold a lighted cigarette up to it to start it). I learned how to go outside the perimeter to answer nature's call (always take your M-16 with you and let your buddies know where you are). I also learned how to set up and take down a mech (a mechanical ambush was a claymore anti-personnel mine hooked to a battery through a trip wire...we called them 'mechs'). Such were the many little nuances of life in the bush. Tim Frater, my squad leader, helped me get squared away. Tim seemed to be a natural at doing this. He was like a teacher...thoughtful and observant. He was in charge, as squad leader, but wanted to be sure I did things the right way. I'm grateful for that.

Each day the platoon would run several patrols along the berms in the Rice Bowl, making our presence known...kind of like the cop on the corner in the neighborhood. David Myers led the first patrol I went on. David struck me as a confident grunt. He seemed to have a good head on his shoulders. I remember my first perception of him was that of a surfer from California. He had bushy blond hair, was tall and lanky (compared to me anyway), and had a great tan. Well, perceptions can often be wrong, and mine were. David (we called him 'My') was a good ol' boy from Virginia, but he was a good grunt. He carried the M-79 as he led us on the patrol. I thought that to be a little strange, but who was I to question others—I had only been in the bush 18 hours. So off I go, following along as 'My' led our patrol. In my imagination, I'm still seeing VC behind every stalk of bamboo. There were a lot of civilians in the Rice Bowl, working their rice paddies and living in their hamlets. The problem was that the VC looked just like civilians. They didn't have uniforms and could easily melt into the local population to prevent being detected. This made the war for grunts much more stressful. Were those women in the rice paddy just working the paddy, or were they plotting their next move against the grunts in their neighborhood? How about that boy leading a water buffalo? Can he be trusted? In time, I learned that the Rice Bowl was really a safe place, and I was very fortunate to begin my tour there. Our patrol was a piece of cake. I'm sure we must have had an area to cover, but I wasn't privy to that kind of stuff. I was really just along for the walk with everyone else. We walked a good ways, stopping at a couple of hooches, checking out a few of the locals, and keeping an eye on things across the rice paddies. Then it was back to the perimeter for a break. Most days, usually late in the afternoon, we would move our perimeter to another location in the Rice Bowl. When not running a patrol there was lots of time for reading, playing cards, cleaning weapons, and writing letters home. I was surprised at the amount of idle time we had. This was not the perception that was presented on the news back home, or in any movies or books I might have seen or read about war; nor was it something that any training prepared me for. The days could be pretty boring; but I was still a newbie and had a lot to learn.

Looks like supper is just about ready. I think this is beans and ham. Note the glow from the C-4 below the cup.

One of the things we did a lot of in our idle time and on patrols was take pictures. We took lots of pictures. Several of the guys, including myself, carried a small camera. On one of our missions, David Bruski even carried a movie camera in his rucksack and took some movies of us humping (hiking) down a creek bed. David was a quick talking guy from Michigan; he was one that was called a "Shake & Bake". He was an 'instant' sergeant that came out of Non-Commissioned Officer (NCO) Training. He had only been with the platoon for about a month when I got there and was one of the squad leaders. David had absorbed his NCO training well and was quite skilled in map reading and calling in support on the radio.

Another attraction in the Rice Bowl was the coke girls. These were young Vietnamese girls who would follow the American troops around (in pacified areas) selling all sorts of things, mostly sodas. I never figured out where they got their stuff, I

A card game in the Rice Bowl. It looks like Pat Byrne (left) is helping a young Vietnamese boy with his cards while a coke girl looks over my shoulder. That's Lonnie Johnson with his back to the camera.

guess the black market; but they always had plenty. And it seemed like there were kids everywhere; they were around a lot of the places we went in the Rice Bowl. If we walked to Highway One (the main north/south route along the coast) to be picked up by trucks, a group of kids and coke girls would always gather while we waited on the trucks. The coke girls would be selling their wares and the kids loved to laugh and carry on, just like kids anywhere. There were adults around too, mostly older, and mostly women. The older adults worked the rice paddies and hauled the rice. I don't remember any young or middle-aged men in the Rice Bowl. I just figured they were with the South Vietnamese Army or the VC, or they were dead.

Carl Groseclose posing next to a group of kids on Highway One.

LZ DEBBIE

For the most part, the people in the Rice Bowl were friendly, and I think they appreciated us being there. They went about their business of life, and we did our job. Our missions in the bush usually lasted 12 days; then we were picked up by helicopters or trucks and taken to LZ (Landing Zone) Debbie for four days of rest and LZ security. The LZ housed artillery and mortar teams, as well as other groups necessary for supporting companies in the bush. The guys on the LZs had it better than the guys in the bush. But the measure of how much better life was for the guy on the LZ than the guy in the bush depended on where a particular LZ was. We grunts knew we were at the bottom of the hill and everything rolled downhill. We didn't care whether the rear guys were in Saigon or on LZ Debbie; they weren't in the bush, and we called them REMF's (Rear Echelon M... F...). As far as I can remember, there was a level of disdain between the two groups. There were about ten rear guys for every one grunt in the field; so I guess we demanded a lot of attention.

On LZ Debbie the platoon was assigned bunkers along the perimeter, and our job was to provide security for the base for four days. We rotated this responsibility with the other companies in the battalion. The perimeter bunkers on Debbie were a two-level creation—the lower level being a sleeping area and the upper level a fighting position. The sleeping area was big enough to hold four to six men in bunk beds; that is, if they could be called beds. Plywood racks would be a better description of these 'beds'. The sleeping area was completely enclosed with no windows, only a door that opened on the side away from the perimeter. The walls of this area would either be plywood on a 2x4 frame covered with sandbags on the outside, or wooden ammo boxes, filled with sand, stacked up. The fighting position—the upper level—was made of half a metal culvert sitting on top of sand-filled ammo boxes, the half-culvert covered with sandbags. The front opening would be walled up with ammo boxes as well, leaving enough room for the occupant to view out and fight, if necessary. Several feet out in front of the perimeter bunker would be a tall chain link fence that formed an arch-shaped barrier of protection against rocket-propelled grenades (RPG). The idea was that if an RPG was fired at the bunker it would detonate in the fence before ever getting to its target. Fortunately, I never got to see this theory tested. There were other bunkers on Debbie that housed the permanent residents there (REMFs)—the tactical operation center (TOC), artillery, communications, clerks, cooks, and all the others. Those bunkers, as I recall, were much stouter and nicer on the inside. But these guys lived on Debbie all the time and wanted as many comforts as could be obtained in such a place. The mess hall on Debbie was also well-sandbagged. A mess hall meant food, so we got hot chow! Hot chow was a good thing!

We got clean clothes (we didn't change in the bush) and showers. The showers were a unique experience. The first step was to take a five-gallon bucket and go get some water. Then you carried the bucket of water up some steps and

LZ Debbie mess hall on the left with a fighting position seen just under the helicopter.

poured it into a large drum on top of the shower stall. Now it was time for the shower. The shower consisted of an on/off spigot that poured water into a coke can that had holes punched in the bottom of it. Turn on the water, get wet. Turn off the water and soap up. Then, turn the water back on and rinse off. I always stood in the shower until all of my five gallons was used up. The water wasn't heated in any way, but who needed 'hot' water in Vietnam? The cold water felt good on a hot Vietnamese day, especially if a breeze was blowing.

At night on LZ Debbie we rotated security with our bunker mates. There was a policy in our area called H&I. It stood for harassment and interdiction. This gave us the freedom to randomly fire our weapons outside the LZ perimeter. Its purpose was to discourage any VC from sneaking up on us. I'm not sure how effective it was, but we enjoyed being able to fire our weapons. One night someone brought in a bunch of M-16 tracer rounds. A tracer is a bullet, like any other bullet, but with an added characteristic. It would be illuminated when fired, being visible on its track to target. We loaded up several magazines with them and proceeded to bounce tracer rounds off the rocks in front of our bunker, creating quite a nice light

On approach to LZ Debbie.(Dale Hill)

show. On another occasion, someone showed up with a case of frags (hand grenades). Like a bunch of kids on the 4th of July, we began tossing frags outside the perimeter. After pulling the pin on the grenade and releasing the spoon (triggering lever) there was supposed to be a four or five-second delay before detonation. That proved to be true, so we began pulling the pin, releasing the spoon, and counting to two before throwing the frag. An entire case of frags didn't last long! As I look back on that experience today, it seems what we were doing was really stupid and dangerous, but at the time it proved to be a lot of fun for a bunch of young grunts.

One time on LZ Debbie an accident did happen. A group of us was at the back of the hill where we could fire our weapons during the day. It was sort of a makeshift firing range. Someone had the M-79 grenade launcher (called the blooper because of the noise it made when it was fired) and was firing HE (high explosive) grenades downrange. I don't know how this happened, but one of the rounds didn't make it downrange. Instead, it hit a metal post in front of the group and detonated. Paul Ashley took a piece of shrapnel in his neck and was hurt really bad. Our medic came up and was helping him, but there was blood everywhere. Doc got Paul stabilized and he was put on a helicopter to the hospital. We never knew what happened to Paul after that—whether he made it or not....

CONNECTIONS WITH THE 'WORLD'

Our days on Debbie were spent listening to music, playing cards (usually Spades), writing letters, and relaxing. We always enjoyed mail call, especially when a 'care package' arrived from the world. We used the word "world" to describe home. Phrases like: "back in the world"; "when I was in the world"; "I heard from the world"; and "I can't wait to get back to the world" were common utterances in the language of the grunt. I have to think it was a reflection of where we were—some place unlike any part of the world we knew. During my tour, I received several of these care packages full of Kool-Aid[1], pudding, and a variety of other goodies. Sometimes one of us would receive something perishable, and it was shared around the squad before it turned green. Other items from care packages were shared too, but I never shared my pudding cups. I remember one package I received had a pack of pudding cups enclosed. I sat and ate every one of those cups of pudding right then and there! They were absolutely the best! Letters were always a treat. There was nothing better than getting news from home. I can still remember the fragrance of Becki's letters. She didn't put perfume or anything on them, but they did have the sweetest smell. And, of course, the news inside the letter was always welcome. At first, because our separation was so fresh, the letters were really special. But later in my tour as home seemed further

---

[1] *Kool-Aid brand material used with permission from Kraft Foods*

and further away, her letters were absolutely the best thing. Of course, I got letters from the rest of the family too. Most of it was just chit-chat family stuff, but on a few occasions my Dad and I exchanged some pretty deep thoughts with each other. I was fortunate to have such support from my family. In addition to the letters from Becki, the two of us exchanged cassette tapes. I had a portable cassette tape player and would record messages to Becki. The tape player was kept secure in Bronco while I was in the bush. On the last day of a mission I would request that the player be brought to the hill. Our guys in the company area (they were REMFs too) did a good job of doing this type of thing for us. At times, some of the other guys in the platoon would join me when I was making a recording, but mostly they were just from me. I would mail these tapes home; after Becki listened to them, she would record a message to send back to me. She also included comments from Chuck, our growing son. I always enjoyed the "goo, goo, goo" he shared. Hearing the voices of those I loved was a huge lift for me in this place, especially later in my tour.

There were many nights on the hill when I could sit in the darkness of the night and just listen to the voice of my love. Those were good moments. Some days in Vietnam were almost unbearable—for a variety of reasons. A letter or cassette tape always brought a connection back to reality and gave reason for hope. I could drift away in my imagination and be reminded of what I had waiting for me. This helped me focus on staying safe and getting home.

Maintaining a connection to the 'world' was a desire that I carried my entire tour. The letters from home really helped, along with the care packages. The tapes that Becki and I exchanged were even more precious because of the sounds of the voices I could hear. Later in my tour, I learned another way to make connection with the 'world' and those I loved and missed. It was the MARS call. MARS (Military Affiliate Radio System, now known as Military Auxiliary Radio System) was a great service provided in Vietnam. MARS was a setup that combined military communication with civilian amateur radio operators around the world. These radio operators would relay a telephone call to a telephone back in the world. The service was free to grunts in 'Nam. There was only one catch. After each statement was made the speaker had to say, "Over"—just like a radio guy would. I remember being on a stand down in Chu Lai when I heard about the MARS opportunity. This was something I wanted to do, so off I went to the MARS station. There was a line of guys ahead of me, but I was willing to wait. I wanted to hear Becki's voice in real time, to tell her how much I loved and missed her and to hear her tell me the same thing. When it was my turn, I stepped into this little booth with a military phone sitting on a small table. The guy in charge let me know what the rules were (saying "over"...), and I gave him the number of home. I hadn't even thought of the time difference between Vietnam and Florida. There was a 12-hour difference in time between the two, and I was calling at 2:00 PM Vietnam time. The reason I know that is because we still laugh about my call waking Becki up at 2:00 AM Florida time! When she came to the phone I said, "Hi Becki, this is Slater calling from Vietnam, over." She responded, "What…why are you calling me at 2:00 in the morning?" and the radio guy who was monitoring the conversation said, "Over". Becki never was one to be 'awake' when she first woke up, and my 2:00 AM interruption of her sleep really messed with her head for a minute. After she realized what was happening, we had a great conversation. We kept forgetting to say "over" though, so the radio guy would slip one in for each of us when we missed it. I mean, really…how do you say, "I love you, over! I miss you, over!"? It was funny, but it was so great! The radio guy must have really enjoyed doing this. Hearing Becki's voice was the sweetest thing for me. The world which, at times in 'Nam, seemed so far away, was still there. Home was STILL THERE. The love was STILL THERE. The call was limited to just a few minutes and—too soon—my time was used up. We said our goodbyes, and I walked out of that booth refreshed and lonely at the same time. I so wanted to keep talking. I wanted to be there with Becki.

It wasn't long before the four days on Debbie were over and we were back out in the bush. This became pretty much routine—12 days in the bush and four days on the hill. Occasionally, we would have a stand down for two or three days, which meant we would come out of the field, usually to Bronco, with no responsibilities at all. It was just a time meant for rest. There was usually some type of entertainment and a lot of down time. If a band came, we always enjoyed the music. If the band was composed of "round eyed girls" (performers from the 'world' instead of locals), we enjoyed the concerts all the more. For some reason we all got kind of 'dreamy eyed' during those times. In addition to the bands and relaxation, there were the doughnut dollies. These were Red Cross girls who came to the rear areas, out to firebases, and even to the bush, to visit the soldiers. They were always present when we had a stand down. These gals were really special and courageous. Why would any girl volunteer to go to a place like Vietnam? They really had a heart for the soldiers. And we soldiers really loved it when they came. Maybe we were thinking of a girl friend or our wife, maybe a sister, but they always brought a thought of home—and that was good. Often they would just mingle in a group of guys, talk, and tell stories; we'd all laugh and dream a little. They always brought happiness with them. They were special.

Ken Cameron getting a Doughnut Dolly doo.

Most of the missions in the bush were the same thing at first, just patrolling the Rice Bowl and making our presence known, and getting resupplied every three days. After a couple of missions, I began getting my bearings and thinking, "I can do this". I was still in my endless tunnel, but no longer alone. I was part of 4th platoon. I didn't feel like a newbie anymore. I was spending 24 hours a day with these guys, learning to trust them and they me. Most days we moved our location; then in the evening we set up our perimeter defenses which consisted of trip flares, claymore mines, and mechs. A trip flare was a flare on a stick. It had a pin in it like a hand grenade. To set up the trip flare, the stick would be stuck in the ground in a semi-concealed area; the pin would be partially pulled out and attached to a piece of fishing line (almost invisible). The line would be stretched across an area of possible approach and secured to a fixed object (usually a small tree or large bush; a small bush wouldn't work because a breeze could move the trip wire and set off the flare). The idea was, if someone approached, the chance was good they would not see the trip wire and would set off the flare, lighting the entire area for several seconds while the flare burned off. This would give us the opportunity to fire them up before they got any closer. The mechs followed the same principle, though they were anti-personnel mines detonated by a blasting cap wired to a battery through a connection made when the trip wire was hit. The claymores were the same anti-personnel mines used in the mechs, but were command-detonated using a clacker (a handheld device that generated an electrical charge strong enough to pop the blasting cap in the claymore).

All of these devices made for a pretty formidable perimeter defense. Everyone knew their field of fire and security responsibility. Each night was the same. When darkness came, all became totally quiet. We would sit, listen, and sleep. Then the sun would come up, and we would wind it up and do it again. One night in the Rice Bowl, one of our mechs detonated. Going from complete silence to the sudden blast of an exploding mech was a rude awakening. Instantly, we were all totally awake and alert. The mech had been set across one of the berms between two rice paddies. We listened; all was quiet. LT called for artillery to pop some illumination rounds so we could see the area. The illumination round would detonate several hundred feet in the air, releasing a flare on a parachute. The parachute allowed the flare time to burn off while it floated slowly to the ground, giving those of us on the ground the light necessary to survey a situation. The flare swinging back and forth from the parachute created some very weird moving shadows on the ground. While using the light of the flare one had to be very careful not to be distracted by these moving shadows. We studied the area of the mech detonation and everything seemed ok, so LT decided to wait until first light to investigate. Some guys went out the next morning and discovered the remains of a frog. Poor critter was apparently just chasing a bug or something and must have hit the trip wire. Another night we got a cat...such was Life in 'Nam!

HILL 56

After several weeks of the Rice Bowl routine, our mission changed a bit. Instead of patrolling the Rice Bowl, we began building an Observation Post (OP) on a small hill in the Rice Bowl. As I recall, this was called Hill 56, and we spent a good part of January there. It was an outpost of bunkers, a mortar pit, and fighting positions that we eventually turned over to the ARVN (Army of the Republic of Vietnam). As I mentioned earlier, the Rice Bowl was a relatively safe area when I was there in 1971. This was because of a lot of hard work and sacrifice by grunts before my arrival. By 1971, the Vietnamization of the war was in full swing. This was the process of American troops interacting more and more with the civilian population, working with the ARVN, and turning military responsibility over to them—especially in areas that were considered pacified, like the Rice Bowl. At the same time, the U.S. was drawing down the number of American troops in the country. Hill 56 was an example of this Vietnamization effort; but, before it could be turned over to the ARVN, the grunts of 4th Platoon had to perform a great deal of manual labor—digging out the fighting positions, building the bunkers, and filling sandbags. This was hot and nasty work. We made sure the ARVN got a respectable place from which they could keep an eye on things.

Completed bunker on Hill 56. (Dale Hill)

Speaking of the ARVN, some folks said they were reputable troops, but my impression of them was not quite as high. We crossed paths with them from time to time during our operations in the Rice Bowl. On one operation, we heard an explosion and went to investigate; it was the ARVN. They were fishing with hand grenades. All these little dead fish were floating in a pool of a creek, and the ARVN guys were scooping them out. And it was the ARVN that ruined my Christmas dinner. We were in the bush on Christmas day, but a cease fire had been declared. Fortunately for us, the cease fire was honored by our enemy. The company was pulled together into one area in the Rice Bowl, along with some of the ARVN troops, to receive a hot meal delivered to us by helicopter.

Groups of men would go to get their hot meal and return with it to their position; then others went to get theirs. It was our time to go get our Christmas meal, so off we went. It was good looking chow...turkey, dressing, potatoes...all sorts of good stuff. I filled my plate full and headed back to our area on the perimeter. While I was returning to my spot, however, some ARVN soldier decided to celebrate the occasion by firing his weapon. Well, what does a grunt do when gun fire happens? Down I went, sprawled on the wet ground (it had been raining). What happened to my Christmas meal? I guess the ants got it. I know I didn't. Several months after we left this AO, we learned that the VC took the OP away from the ARVN. That was life in 'Nam...and that was my exposure to the ARVN.

The OP was well-positioned to keep an eye on the Rice Bowl, as well as the mountains at the bowl's edge. Once the OP was completed we stayed there a bit, and I remember there was a 50-caliber machine gun set up with a starlight scope on it. A starlight scope was the first generation of night vision equipment. It multiplied the available light through the scope to make things visible, though everything appeared green. Just before dawn one morning, some members of our battalion's SRRP (short range recon patrol) team were present. One of them, using the starlight scope on the 50-cal., spotted some VC moving in the area. The gunner opened up on them. Then the SRRP team went out to take a look at the area and reported finding only a foot. I guess the leg that went with the foot got away. It wasn't long before we turned the OP over to the ARVN and were back in the bush.

Tom Duran checking out the 50- Caliber Machine Gun on the OP.
(Dale Hill)

The missions returned to what we previously knew, and things were picking up a bit in and around the Rice Bowl. 4th Platoon and other elements of Bravo Company began reporting an increase in visual sightings of VC in our area. The Rice Bowl, being mostly pacified, was fairly safe in the daytime, but the night belonged to the VC. That is when most of these sightings usually occurred—in late afternoon or right after sundown. When the enemy was spotted, it was usually at a distance and artillery was called in on the enemy location. Then the following morning a patrol would be sent out to check the area. Usually very little, if anything, was found. Occasionally we might find a weapon left behind or a pack with blood on it. Also during this time we, and other platoons, began finding more stashes of supplies; and sometimes we found well-hidden tunnels or hiding places. The tunnels were usually small and could be easily destroyed with some C-4. All of these encounters sharpened our awareness of our surroundings. Things seemed just a bit more serious than when I first arrived.

One afternoon our platoon had already established our night perimeter, and we were making ready for the night when a call came for us to prepare for a CA (combat assault by helicopter) to provide assistance to a sister platoon. We were all business, not knowing exactly what was ahead for us, but knowing it must be pretty serious. The situation was this: our CP Platoon (Command platoon with company commander), 2nd Platoon, and our SRRP Team were in close proximity to each other with CP and 2nd Platoons on the same ridge line. CP Platoon had been moving on this ridge to a new night location when 2nd Platoon spotted a much larger force of VC or NVA (North Vietnamese Army) several hundred meters away walking a trail in the valley below them. The enemy was moving in the direction of the 2nd Platoon. CP Platoon quickly reversed their move and pushed hard to an area near where 2nd Platoon was, which was much more defendable and had room for a LZ. SRRP was directed to move in the direction of the approaching enemy to set up an ambush, but with events happening really fast there wasn't time; it was decided to reverse them to join with 2nd Platoon. The enemy line was weighed down with heavy packs, weapons, and at least one mortar tube. The estimated size of the element ranged from 35 to 80, depending on who you talked to. Artillery was called in on them; then gunships came in on them, strafing them and hitting them with rockets. It had gotten dark by this time, and one of the choppers carried a spotlight that was used to light up the enemy below. There were reports of many enemy casualties in the area. All of this was wrapping up just as we were dropped in at the CP Platoon's location, to reinforce them. I was on the last chopper to arrive and, by that time, it was totally dark—black dark. I was sitting in the door of the chopper and couldn't see a thing on the ground. I couldn't even see the ground...just pitch black darkness. Then, as the pilot maneuvered his chopper into position to land, I saw a light flashing on the ground and watched in amazement as the chopper pilot placed the nose of the helicopter on the flashing strobe light in the darkened landing zone. These were the days before fully functioning night vision gear, and that chopper pilot was relying on the grunt on the ground to be in the right spot. As soon as we jumped out, the chopper was out of there. Our squad was told we were going down a trail outside of the perimeter to set up a night ambush. Oh joy! This was the trail that the enemy would be coming up if they wanted to meet us. And we had no idea what the surrounding area was like since it was already dark!

A night ambush was a scary thing. I went on a few of these during my tour. It consisted of a small group of guys, usually a squad, going outside of the platoon perimeter after dark. The ambush site would normally have been checked out during the day, but not set up until after dark. The site was usually along a trail or open area of suspected enemy movement. Sometimes a mech or two would be set up, or some claymores would be placed in front of the ambush position. Most of the time, however, the small group would just melt into the darkness of the brush at the site and, as quietly as possible, take up positions fairly close to each other. We used touch to communicate and to make sure we were each still awake. Such was the situation that night on the ridge. No sleep was had on this night. Every little noise, whether a breeze blowing the brush we hid in, or an animal scurrying along the ground, got our full attention. Thankfully it was an uneventful night, and the sun came up again just like it had every other morning. We walked back up the trail to the perimeter and, for the first time, I saw the landing zone that the helicopter had landed in the night before. It was incredibly small. I don't know how the helicopter was able to fit in. That pilot had exercised some real skill to put the chopper down safely; and he had displayed a lot of trust in the man who held the strobe light.

We learned that, while we remained in our position on the ridge, 2nd Platoon and SRRP team would move into the area from their location and investigate the results of the engagement the night before. Lots of 'stuff' and blood splatters were found, but no enemy. Apparently the enemy had dropped much of their gear so they could remove their killed and wounded from the scene. It took three helicopters to haul all of their stuff back to Duc Pho.

Many years later, at one of our reunions, I learned the rest of the story about this incident. Tim Frater, my original squad leader, had moved to the CP Platoon before the time of the incident. He carried the battalion radio for the company commander. Tim related his memory of that night at our first reunion. After 4th Platoon had joined the CP platoon, battalion was requesting that a patrol be sent down into the valley to engage any enemy there. Our company commander, Lt. Kroeger, didn't want to do this. He wanted to wait until daylight, but battalion insisted. Kroeger, knowing that battalion monitored all radio traffic, got 4th Platoon's radio guy (RTO) to move to the opposite side of our joint perimeter and then the CP RTO and our RTO communicated back and forth as if a patrol was moving down into the valley, reporting back negative results. When this story was told at our reunion, many of us were moved by our CO's actions. Unfortunately, LT Kroeger passed away in 1993 and we were not able to thank him for most likely saving some lives that night. After hearing this story about LT Kroeger watching out for his troops, I couldn't help but think that he must have had a huge influence on the leadership below him. LT Vince Varel and later, LT David Olender, who replaced LT Varel at some point in the spring of 1971, both kept their men safe. From the view of this lowly grunt, they—along with the squad leaders of the platoon—did an excellent job doing so. Two of the squad leaders were David Bruski and Darrel Fuhs. Darrel was one of several guys from Wisconsin in 4th Platoon. He took Tim Frater's (also from Wisconsin) place as my squad leader when Tim moved to CP. Darrel was a little weird and maybe that's why I liked him so much. I think I was a little weird, too. Darrel did a good job as squad leader. There was also Sergeant Kirwan. He was a lifer, an old timer who had some history with the Army. He seemed to always keep to himself. We called him "Super Six" because he was a staff sergeant, or E-6. 4th Platoon's other leaders were Michael Gatewood, David Myers, and Kent Swanson, all sergeants. None of our leaders took foolish chances that I ever saw. They were careful with their responsibility, and I have always been grateful for that.

INTO THE MOUNTAINS

It wasn't long before our missions began to change again and become more serious. I guess we had officially turned over the Rice Bowl to the ARVN, because we moved out of the Rice Bowl and into the foothills around the bowl. Things were different here. This was known as a free-fire zone, which meant, if anything moved, we could shoot it. The scary part was they would shoot back. There were supposed to be no civilians in this area. We became much more cautious.

Instead of walking along berms in the rice paddies we were climbing mountains, crossing rivers and swamps, cutting trail with machetes, loaded down with 60 or 70 pounds of gear, all the while trying to be quiet and find the enemy. I never understood how we could be whacking through the jungle with machetes and expect to sneak up on the enemy; but on we went. Each day, as we cut trail and patrolled, LT would decide the location of our night perimeter. Then, late in the afternoon, we would go into that area and get settled for the night. Usually claymores were strategically set up outside our perimeter. Mechs would be set out on the path we made to reach our perimeter; and if there were trails in the area, a mech or two might be put out on them. Trip flares would also be set up.

One of the other changes that took place in this new environment was how we slept. In the Rice Bowl the only option was on the ground—maybe on an air mattress, but still on the ground. Once we got into the jungle, some of us began sleeping in hammocks. Our hammocks were made from our poncho liner and tied to trees with spare boot strings. Sounds crazy but it worked, and it was good sleeping! The poncho liner was a great piece of gear. It was like a very lightweight blanket that was designed to attach to a poncho with little ties along its edge. It was strong and warm and, if wet, would dry in a very short time. One advantage of sleeping in the poncho liner hammock was that it provided a way to avoid the mosquitos. The edge of the poncho liner had little ties that

Here is a picture of me getting my boots on before rolling out in the morning.

matched the holes in the poncho. The tie worked really good, making a cocoon. I would tie a canteen to the tie in the middle of the side of the liner/hammock and, when I got into the hammock, I would then flip the canteen over me. Its weight would hold the liner in a cover over me while I slept; it worked great. I would lie there and listen to the mosquitos hitting the outside, trying to get in, as I drifted off to sleep. And hit they did; there would be the unmistakable buzz of an approaching mosquito, then a light 'thump' on the outside of my hammock. The mosquitos were unbearable at night, and the hammock proved a good defense against them. And, there was no problem getting out of the hammock quickly if the need arose. This was proved one night, later in my tour, when some firing began. I just rolled over, fell out of the hammock, and was immediately on the ground with my weapon, ready for whatever might come my way!

Walking in Vietnam. Someone was up front cutting trail. That's Dale Doege behind me. That ruck sack on my back weighed in well above 50 pounds.

Working in the jungle was different from the Rice Bowl in other ways, too. Visibility in the jungle was limited by the thick undergrowth. This required us to always be vigilant about our surroundings. In the Rice Bowl, most of the time we could see several hundred yards in all directions, but in the jungle that distance was cut down to just a few feet. Part of being always vigilant was maintaining noise discipline both night and day...except, of course, for that machete. All conversations were at a whisper; and everything we did: setting up or tearing down our perimeter; setting out or picking up night defenses; cleaning weapons; or playing cards—everything was done with being quiet in mind. The jungle also proved to be really dark at night. It had been dark in the Rice Bowl, but we could still see by light of the moon and the stars. In the jungle there was nothing but darkness. In the Rice Bowl, on a clear night I could see silhouette shapes of things. In the jungle, I could see nothing, not even my hand in front of my face. There was one thing we could see though...the rotting material on the ground gave off an iridescent light that glowed in the darkness. In some places the floor of the jungle would be speckled with this weird glow. The total darkness brought about some changes in how we conducted our nights. Security would begin, as always, at first dark; but in the jungle, all we did was pass a watch around the perimeter. There was nothing to watch, nothing to see—unless, of course, a trip flare went off. If that happened, everyone was awake. Passing the watch was simple and quiet. Quiet was good, real good. So, the night of 10-12 hours (from sundown to sunrise) would be divided among 12 grunts, resulting in no more than an hour's security each night. This was a lot better than security on the hill with the night being divided among 3-6 men. We slept more in the bush because there was nothing to do after dark except sleep or keep watch. I hated the last hour of the night. It seemed daylight would never arrive. When I had this hour I would watch as the darkness would begin to change into daylight. It was oh so slow. Things would begin to take shape around the perimeter, and I would sit in my hammock waiting for the hour to be over. Sometimes, as the shapes became visible, they looked suspicious and had to be studied carefully. In darkness, when looking at shapes, they disappear when you look straight at them. We had been taught to look on either side of an object—back and forth—to get a good view of it. This worked, and I would use the technique as the black darkness began to fade into shapes. Lighter and lighter it would come until dawn and the last hour of watch was over. When the hour was over, though, everyone else was still asleep. There was no one to wake up for the next turn, and there was nothing to do but wait until everyone was awake. If we had something planned early that day, then the last guy started waking everyone else up. If it was a normal day, everyone rolled out as they awoke. The last hour could sometimes end up being thirty minutes to an hour longer; but guys would begin to stir and begin the day, still at a whisper...always at a whisper. C-4 would be cranked up to cook the morning C-ration; guys would step out of the perimeter to relieve themselves; then we would begin to gather things up and prepare for our day's move.

An example of some of what we experienced. This is me crossing a river in front of Dale Hill and the rest of the platoon.

I remember on one occasion, after the sun had come up and we were packing up preparing to move, Pat Byrne and I were out to retrieve one of the claymore anti-personnel mines we used around our night perimeter. Pat (we called him "Stubby") was the life of the party when we were on the hill, but could take care of business in the bush. On the hill, Pat and his buddy Carl Groseclose (we called him "Boo") were inseparable. There was usually a crowd around them and lots of music and laughter going on. I learned they were buddies before 'Nam and had stuck together all the way to 'Nam. In my experience that was very unusual. That morning in the bush, Pat had his M-16, and I was rolling up the wire to the claymore. We were in a meadow, at the edge of the jungle where our night perimeter was, above a stream that ran on

75

the other side of a growth of bushes. The only noise that could be heard was the bubbling of the water in the stream as it ran over the rocks lying in its bed. As we turned to move back to the perimeter, we noticed movement in the creek. There was a small gap in the bushes along the creek, and we saw 3 VC walking down the creek. They were already past us and we hadn't seen or heard them, nor had they seen or heard us. The bushes between the meadow and the creek had visually shielded us from each other. This was spooky. We quickly returned to the perimeter and told LT. He got the map out, plotted their assumed travel down the creek, and called in artillery on their suspected location. The sound of artillery being fired, coming in, and detonating is something I'll always remember. We would hear the artillery guys on the radio say, "Shot out" meaning their howitzer or mortar had just fired. Then a few seconds later we would hear this low, thump sound for each shot being made. This was the sound of the shot reaching our ears. Then there was the screeching sound (similar to a jet), rapidly approaching, and then the detonation. It could get pretty noisy if there were a lot of shots and the target was close by. We heard the shots coming in as we finished gathering our stuff. Then we loaded up, and headed down the creek after the VC. We found nothing. We continued to move in the same direction the VC had been moving, but left the creek and walked in the jungle and brush alongside the creek. I was walking toward the back of the platoon when the lead element walked up on twelve VC taking a break in some trees. Our approach had been heard by the VC and they were scrambling to escape the area. The lead squad, with Ken Sciford on the M-60 machine gun, quickly got on line and opened up on them as they moved forward through the trees. The sudden break of the silence by the gunfire sent the rest of the platoon to the ground. We didn't know what was going on in front of us at that moment, but we were on full alert, looking in all directions. After just a few seconds the firing stopped, and LT called us all up to form a perimeter and take inventory of some captured stuff. In their haste to escape, the VC had left behind 1 AK47, 15 grenades, 12 hammocks, 100 pounds of rice, and 100 pounds of salt. Then someone discovered a blood trail so we knew the lead squad had inflicted damage on our enemy. LT called me and two other guys, and told us to follow the blood trail. So, off we went. We were all really tense in a good sort of way—alert—careful, not knowing what we would find. The blood went off across a grassy area, into the woods to a trail, and then up a hill on the trail. We began to follow the blood. I was in the lead and was moving really slow, checking out every step. What if the wounded guy was waiting for us with his own AK-47? What if he came back toward us and hid in ambush after leaving blood for us to follow? What if...what if...what if...? Slowly, quietly we continued up the trail. Our senses were all on full alert, listening, watching...even smelling. Then there was no more blood. What did this mean? Did the guy just vanish? Did he get help? How many were out there? Where were they? We pushed on a little further, finding no evidence of the enemy, and then turned to go back to our perimeter. That's when we heard more gunfire at the perimeter. When we got back we learned that one of the VC had circled around and come back into the area from a different direction; he was crawling toward the platoon with a grenade in one hand and a knife in the other. Tom Duran, who was pulling security on the perimeter, had spotted him and fired him up. Tom was a good guy. I got to know Tom within just a few days of my arrival to 4th Platoon. We enjoyed each other's company. Tom was a quiet sort, almost studious, but he had a good sense of humor. Tom had done his job that day. He stayed alert and saved some lives in 4th Platoon. It was the same every day. We had to do our jobs, staying alert, because we never knew what might happen. If Tom had been lax, some in 4th Platoon would have surely been hurt that day, maybe killed. I had been with 4th Platoon right at three months when this happened; this event was my first experience with actual combat. It was fast, loud, and then it was over in seconds. I had just reacted in the middle of an adrenaline rush. I guess training was paying off. As it was happening I didn't even think 'scary'; after it was over it was scary, but I blew it off. If I had taken time to sit and process everything in my head, I probably would have quickly become a basket case. As it was, we just moved on and, as we often said in 'Nam, "It don't mean nothing"....this was the way we moved on from such an event. Shortly after the VC was killed by Tom, a sister platoon came into our area to join us, and a resupply chopper came out with fresh ammo and retrieved the captured stuff. Then it was back to normal, if there was such a thing as normal in 'Nam.

LEARNING TO RELAX

There were many of these 12-day missions in the bush, filled with the ever present stress of alertness required by our situation. I remember being more tired than scared. I became accustomed to the possibility of conflict, and that awareness was always present. I believe anyone who has ever been in a combat situation knows of this state of alertness. In all we did, 24 hours a day, for each 12-day mission, I was always on edge—my senses were always on alert. It began the moment I stepped off the chopper in the LZ at the beginning of each mission, and it didn't end until I was back on the hill. Even in the worst exhaustion, it seemed I could quickly react if the need arose; but we still had to keep on the move, fighting the terrain and the heat. Many times a five-minute break would be the best thing that could happen. Maybe LT would want to send someone ahead a short distance to look at something, or make a map check or radio check; or maybe we just stopped for a water break. Whatever the reason, we would just sit down where we stopped, lean against our rucksacks, drink some water, and rest. On longer breaks, it was easy to catch a few minutes of sleep. Well, at least the eyes got closed. We always knew that someone, usually the point guy and the last guy in line, were keeping their eyes on things for the rest of us. Then it was back to it. It seemed like a never-ending pursuit of the other side of the mountain. When we would finally set up a perimeter in the late afternoon, I remember using the underbrush a lot of times to hang my shirt, towel, and even bush hat on, so they could all dry from the sweat they were soaked with.

Lonnie Johnson taking a break on his rucksack.

There were also times of sitting and relaxing in a quiet place...maybe waiting to move to a night perimeter, or to a landing zone for resupply every third day. These were times for reading or napping, writing a letter home, or maybe even playing a quiet game of spades. Quiet was the key word. Always quiet, except for that crazy machete chopping trail.

It was during these quiet moments of rest that I began to pick up on some of Lonnie Johnson's artistic work. Lonnie (we called him "Flash") was quite the accomplished artist. He would sketch different things, but often created colorful

80

designs with the colored pens he carried in the ammo can in his rucksack. He also kept a sketch diary of his tour. Sadly, someone stole the diary out of Lonnie's rucksack just before a stand down. He was really hurt by that. It would have been a treasure. I began watching Flash, and then began borrowing his pens to "paint up" the envelopes of the letters I was sending home. Lonnie was great about that, loaning me his pens and even giving me suggestions on my "artwork". I never asked the folks what they thought of my colorful envelopes. They were probably thinking I was going off the deep end...

One of the envelopes I colored up before mailing.

Then there were the times to take a bath. Yep, we did that from time to time. It was a good day when a patrol would return to our day perimeter and report they had found a nice creek with a swimming hole in an area we could secure. We would load up and move to the location. Security assignments would be made, and a few of us at a time would strip and take the plunge. It was great!

One of our many swimming holes.

Descriptions of my life in Vietnam would not be complete without mentioning the weather. The weather in Vietnam could be summed up in just a few words: hot, humid, and wet. Often these all got mixed in together to make life just plain miserable. It seemed like it was always hot—really hot. I adjusted, but I don't think I ever got used to it. Doc always made sure we took our salt tablets and drank plenty of water—Eli Williams was our medic. We all called him 'Doc'. He was the best. He took great care of us in all situations. He was always checking on us to be sure we were ok, and he knew his stuff.

Doc—Eli Williams (Dale Hill)

Because it was always hot, the rain wasn't too bad...at first; but when it kept raining—all the time—and never stopped— well...what can I say?! We were just wet...<u>all</u> <u>the</u> <u>time</u>. We slept wet. We walked wet. We patrolled wet. We waited wet. We wrote letters wet. We played cards wet. We were just wet.

LT had stopped our movement to send a couple of guys ahead to check things out. I took Dale's M-16 and asked him to take this picture. It's pouring rain. Nobody wanted to sit down in the mush so we just all stood in the rain.

There was one time we walked out of the mountains and across the Rice Bowl as we were coming in from a mission. It had rained maybe the entire time, and the temperatures were cooler than the normal hot. We had moved close to Highway One and would be picked up the next day on the highway by trucks, to be taken to LZ Debbie. We were soaked; our skin was wrinkled up from all the wet. Everyone was miserable. We set up our perimeter for the night and began our nightly routine. I remember lying on the ground, wrapped in my poncho liner, under my poncho trying to sleep, but only shivering. Did I say we were miserable? I recall we did something before daylight that happened only once, and I've never known any others that did this on their tours. We built a fire—a nice fire...so much for light discipline! I think the logic was this: we were in the Rice Bowl, which was pretty safe; we were miserable and cold (really cold); and if we felt like this, then any red-blooded Viet Cong would be smart enough to stay in his cave or hooch. It was probably not the best thing we could have done, but it did provide us some temporary relief and thankfully led to no problems.

Then there was the mission when we were told a typhoon was going to hit Vietnam and we needed to be sure we were on high ground. We moved to high ground and set up a perimeter, each of us under his poncho in an effort to stay dry. We would use extra boot strings to suspend the poncho from bushes or trees to create a low shelter. Our efforts to stay dry, however, were pretty much wasted. Then we learned the helicopters couldn't fly because of the weather, and we would not be getting our normal three-day resupply. We had to make do with what we had. I think the resupply was delayed a couple of days. I just remember when the resupply finally came, I was down to one can of C-Ration peanut butter, a can of crackers, and almost out of water; though with the rain like it was, water was not a big problem. Beans and ham (not my favorite C-ration) never looked so good!

Resupply would normally come every three days with a stack of C-Ration cases, mail, fresh water, and any other material we might need. Letters from home were read and then destroyed to prevent personal information from falling into enemy hands. The C-Ration cases contained several individual meals and were distributed to the squads; then the contents were divided up by each man making one choice followed by each of the squad members. We followed that pattern until everything was passed out. Each meal contained a can of 'main course' and some 'sides'. Sometimes the 'sides' were a can of crackers or peanut butter or jelly. There was also hot chocolate mix, instant coffee, sugar, salt, pepper, plastic utensils, cigarettes, toothpaste, and P-38 can openers. Once everything was distributed, sometimes we would have a 'swap meet' to exchange stuff with each other to obtain our favorite meal or side. My favorite boxes were the meals with a can of peaches or a can of pound cake. I also liked the chicken and rice meal, but the peaches and pound cake mixed together made a very nice treat!

A typical resupply scene. The helicopter didn't like to hang around too long, so it was all hustle.

We would use the cardboard from the large C-Ration case to make a nice cushion in the frame of our rucksacks. Anything left unused was buried. We also always buried empty C-Ration cans after each meal. The VC were notorious for finding stuff and using it in some way—a C-Ration can filled with explosive could make a nasty booby trap. Plus, burying everything made it more difficult for the VC to know exactly where we had been.

It was during my tour in Vietnam that I learned to drink coffee, but my coffee then was modified more than the cup of black coffee I drink today. I would start with a canteen cup of water, light up some C-4 plastic explosive to cook with on my little stove made from a small C-Ration can I had previously emptied, or a ring of small stones. Once I got the water heated to my satisfaction, I would then add instant coffee, creamer, sugar, and a bag of hot chocolate mix. This was my morning 'brew'—it went great with peaches and pound cake. Of course, the cooking method was the same for any of the C-Rations. That's the only reason we carried C-4, except for those occasional times when we needed to blow something up. Great cooking fuel! On a few missions, we received some freeze-dried meals that were the precursor to the MREs the military uses today. They were pretty good, and much lighter than C-Ration cans.

My breakfast table with a full cup of my 'brew'. The ammo can was water proof when sealed and a safe place to carry things that needed to stay dry.

PROTESTS AND FRUSTRATIONS

During my tour we were always keeping up with the news from home. Whether it was the local ball team or national headlines, we tried to stay abreast of what was going on. Vietnam was always in the news. Vietnam was the first TV war, and for many in America this was the way they knew what was going on, though what was broadcast was always filtered through the editor's choice. Becki spent her evenings with Walter Cronkite and CBS News to stay up on things. We grunts knew that there was a lot of controversy back in the states about the Vietnam War, and this was a point of discussion for some of us. Recently I was reading through the letters I had written to my parents during my tour (they had saved them all, and given them to me upon my return). As I read them I was reminded of my disgust with the protesters back home. It seemed to me that the soldiers in Vietnam were the last thing on anyone's mind. I had expressed my frustrations to my Dad on a few occasions. In one letter, when talking about the protestors, I wrote,

> "Several of us were talking last night about the war, demonstrations, etc. Well, I've had this feeling for a long time but being over here on the other side it really stings. Being over here is bad enough. I could have gone to jail or Canada, but why run? Sometimes now I wish I had. It hurts to read the papers and hear of the demonstrations and riots for <u>peace</u> where people and property are being destroyed. It hurts to

see a crowd of people waving the VC flag or communist flag when you know guys over here are being hurt by that 'flag' every day. It hurts to hear of groups sending...money to N. Vietnam. These are all minority groups but they make it big. Sure, they want us out, maybe. We want out too. More than they know. I think what hurts most of all, above the demonstrations, riots, flag waving and aid, is the way some of our country's "fearless leaders" are "playing" with us over hear (sic)..."

My letter went on with more of my frustrations and hurts. Then I asked Dad, "...wonder if you could write somebody and just tell 'em..." Well, my Dad did just that. He composed a letter to Senator Talmadge (Georgia) and President Nixon expressing my feelings about things, and apparently included my letter, or a portion of it. I really appreciated him doing that, as well as the response he received back from the President. Dad gave me the President's letter when I returned home, and I still have it today. (When I pulled the president's letter out to review for this writing I noticed for the first time that it had been written on my birthday. I wondered if that was intentional...I chuckled...)

Slater Davis

THE WHITE HOUSE

WASHINGTON

The Western White House
San Clemente

July 13, 1971

Dear Mr. Davis:

It was thoughtful of you to take the time to write
recently, and I am grateful for your kindness in
sending your son's letter to me.

You may be sure that I share his concern for the
effects demonstrations at home have on the situation abroad. Our men deserve the best of us, and
as a nation, we bear a very special responsibility
to those who are serving in Vietnam. I, too, feel
it is a minority making these headlines, but we must
all make it our job to see that the spirits of our
servicemen are not dampened by headlines at home.

I am enclosing copies of a speech I made at West
Point recently in which I tried to cover this theme,
and I hope you will want to send it along to Slater.

With my appreciation and best wishes to you and
your family,

Sincerely,

Richard Nixon

The Reverend C. Edward Davis
Lawrenceville Presbyterian Church
Decatur Highway
Lawrenceville, Georgia 30245

Letter to my Dad from President Nixon.

My experience in Vietnam, and my reactions to those who protested while we were there, impacted me in many ways. My heart goes out to active duty guys and gals today as they go into harm's way. And I am always angered by those who protest and complain when our nation's best are 'standing on the wall' for the rest of us. I have never been able to wrap my head around such a lack of gratitude. And, as it was when I was in 'Nam, my greatest disgust comes when our political leaders play politics with the men and women who have sworn to protect and defend our Constitution—thus our way of life. In recent years our military has regained a place of respect and honor that was missing in my experience during the Vietnam era and the years that followed it. Once again we remember Veterans Day and Memorial Day for what they really are, and troops can wear their uniforms in public without worrying about being verbally or physically attacked by those they protect. It is always heartwarming for me today to see how America treats her soldiers.

Slater Davis

Some of my attitude and emotions found their way into some simple poetry while I was in 'Nam. Examples of these verses are included here.

CLOSER TO HOME
(Written by Slater Davis
in Vietnam, 1971)

I walk through the jungle with squad and platoon,
I sleep in the jungle with hopes for a moon.
I spend 12 months with other guys alone,
And each day, each night we're closer to home.
Our life goes on day after day,
We do our job in our own special way.
We go over the mountain like a fine tooth comb.
And each day, each night we're closer to home.
Sometimes we wonder whether it's right or it's wrong.
Nothing we can do, 'cept keep walking along.
The life of a grunt seems always alone.
Wonder if we'll ever be gettin' back home?

TIME PASSES ON
(Written by Slater Davis
in Vietnam, 1971)

Time passes on, the men come and go.
Time passes on, it'll never slow.
For years they have come to serve their time,
It's a job that's unbearable to any mind.
They hump and they dig, they sweat and fight,
Their job is filled with love, hate and fright.

Time passes on, the men come and go.
Time passes on it'll never slow.
A love for their buddies and for life,
A love for the "world" and a lonely wife.

A hate for the lifers, their orders and rules,
A hate for the jungle, it's hot and so cruel.

A fright of the enemy, his coolness and tricks,
Keeps the men going through the sticks.

Time passes on, the men come and go.
Time passes on, it'll never slow.

They hump through the paddies and over a hill,
Many are out there against their will.
The young men, our future, were too good to lie,
Now they're in 'Nam and some will soon die.

Time passes on, the young men they send.
Time passes on, when will it all end?

THANKS AMERICA!
(Written by Slater Davis
in Vietnam, 1971)

Thanks, oh America for caring for us.
You are really good people, in thee do we trust!

In thee do we trust, HA! What a joke!
You don't give a damn if we live or we croak!
Your flags are all waving, not Red, White and Blue,
The flags you are waving are VC and gook!

You say stop the war for the GI's are dying,
But you know way down deep that you're really lying.

The war would have been over by now, my dear friends
If you hadn't been yelling like a bunch of crazed fiends.

SAN JUAN HILL

In April of 1971, we learned that our Area of Operations (AO) was changing again. LZ Debbie was being closed and we were moving to Fire Support Base (FSB) San Juan Hill (SJH). SJH was further west, away from the coast and civilization. It was located on top of a tall mountain, over 1,000 feet high, and only accessible by helicopter or on foot. From SJH one had a commanding view of the surrounding mountains and valleys. On a clear day one could see the Rice Bowl and FSB Bronco on the coast of the South China Sea. Dale Doege joined 4th Platoon right after we moved to SJH. Dale was another addition to 4th Platoon from Wisconsin and he talked in a slow, drawn out, Wisconsin way. If he hadn't had that weird way of pronouncing words, I would have thought he was from around Georgia somewhere. He and I struck a chord and became pretty close. He was one of the guys that contributed voices on some of the cassette tapes I sent home to Becki.

One of our first missions from SJH began by Bravo Company walking off the hill. This was Dale's first mission. This was a tough walk for all of us, but it was a killer for Dale. Just picture a mountain you are familiar with that is steep, full of vegetation, and creeks filled with huge boulders. Now, imagine walking down the side of that mountain on a trail that has just been cut by someone in front of you, and then down the creeks, with 60 or 70 pounds on your back, always with the possibility of the VC or NVA taking a shot at you. Along the way Darrel Fuhs saw that Dale was struggling. He took M-60 ammo from Dale's rucksack and put on his own rucksack. A bit later Darrel took Dale's claymore and clacker. That's the kind of man Darrel was—a great squad leader. Once we got into the valley and the creek was leveling out and becoming wider, we began looking for a nice pool to cool off in. Not Dale; he just wanted to crash. Dale told me later he was 'done'! He didn't care if the VC jumped out and shot him right then and there. He didn't care what happened. Fortunately for Dale—and for us—the enemy was nowhere to be seen that day. Dale survived his first day and the rest of his tour. So began another 12-day mission in the bush. The entire company moved into the valley below SJH and then split up into platoons to cover different areas of the terrain.

A picture of one side of San Juan Hill. Here a Chinook helicopter is delivering water. The South China Sea can be seen in the distance on the right side of the photo.

Walking the creek at the bottom of San Juan Hill. That's me in the foreground.
(Dale Doege)

Our missions in this AO consisted of lots of hacking trail through thick jungle, though some of our movement did not require this. We all took turns walking point. Walking point meant you were the first guy in line. This was a vulnerable spot and carried a lot of responsibility. The point man was the most exposed if the enemy was discovered, or if a booby trap lay in the platoon's path. A booby trap could be a covered pit filled with sharpened sticks called punji sticks, or some type of explosive device placed along the route of movement. The punji sticks were made of bamboo, sharpened to a fine point, and then hardened over a fire. The ends would often be coated in human waste to cause infection in the wound received when one fell through the covering over the pit. Explosive devices could be set along a trail or other strategic location, detonated by trip wire or some other type of trigger device. The VC were very creative with their booby traps. The booby traps were designed to maim and kill, causing many of the wounds and deaths in Vietnam. The enemy would often leave subtle markers along a trail to indicate a device was set ahead. This would alert their own people to "go around" the area. This was one of the things a point man watched for, keeping a sharp eye on the path we were using for anything out of the ordinary. This, however, took the point man's eyes off the long-range view, increasing vulnerability. The long-range view became the job of the second man in line, or the 'slack man'. As the point man surveyed the path just in front of the platoon, the slack man would be looking ahead, down the trail or through the brush, for any sign of the enemy. A good point man was invaluable to a platoon, and a good slack man was a point man's best friend. In the areas of thick brush the point man was the one who cut the trail for the rest of the guys to follow. Some of the guys seemed to enjoy walking point. Though I took my turns at walking point and hacking away with my machete, I never liked it. The only wounds I received in 'Nam came from my well-sharpened machete. On two different occasions, I swung down on a large vine only to find that the vine was hollow and the machete made it all the way to my leg. One time I whacked my calf pretty good; on the other occasion I sliced open my knee. I felt pretty stupid, not to mention the pain in my leg. Doc patched me up as best he could, and someone else took over cutting trail each time

On another mission, as I was chopping away, I noticed a leech on me after we had gone through some brush in a marshy area. Leeches were not uncommon in our AO. One of our guys even woke up one morning with one on the roof of his mouth. Well, I see this leech on me and grab my bug juice to squirt him to get him to fall off. Then I see another leech, then another. That particular time, as I was walking point and chopping trail, I had walked right through a "leech village". They were all over me and Dale Doege, who was walking slack. Doc had us strip down to our birthday suits and began to work on removing the leeches and bandaging us up. The leech would inject an anti-coagulant to prevent the blood from clotting and, as Doc got the leeches off me, there were little trickles of blood flowing from each of the bites. I must have been quite a sight. Doc changed each of the gauze pads on me three times before the bleeding stopped. I haven't liked leeches since. Ugly little buggers!

This new AO was a lot different from the area in and around the Rice Bowl. The terrain was tougher, and the occupants were not sociable. We were spending our time in their neighborhood now, instead of among the friendlies in the Rice Bowl area. When it was time to pay them a visit, the most common way of reaching them was by helicopter. The combat assault by helicopter (CA) proved to be an effective and quick way to get troops to a destination in Vietnam. When the choppers came in to pick us up, six or seven guys would clamber aboard. The two guys on each side would sit in the door with their feet hanging over the skids of the helicopter. I always enjoyed this ride, even when we were coming into an

Loading up for the next CA. (Dale Hill)

area pretty fast. I got some wind in my face; got a good view of the countryside and of the landing zone; and I was the only guy in the way of me getting out and onto the ground. Sometimes those chopper pilots wanted to get in and out real fast and wasted no time getting into a landing zone. On such occasions, the pilot would often take a hard turn as he entered his approach. Doing this would turn the chopper virtually on its side in midair. If he stopped right then, everyone would fall out; but the physics of it all, because he kept moving, held us in place. I can remember more than once sitting in the door of the chopper, looking straight ahead, and all that was in view was the ground. Fortunately for everyone on board, the pilot would straighten out and we would land right side up.

Pickups could be an adrenaline rush, too. Maybe it was a small LZ or the reports of enemy in the area—who knows. Sometimes those gutsy chopper pilots would get airborne just a few feet, then drop the nose of the chopper. This enabled the pilot to quickly accelerate out of the area, all while staying fairly close to the ground until he got his bird up to a decent speed to ascend to a cruising altitude. For any grunt, the 'thump, thump, thump' of the chopper became a welcomed sound. I find that even today, when I hear that sound, my head turns towards it, to catch a glimpse of the chopper. I don't know how many of these CAs I took during my tour, but it was plenty. And every one of them was better than humping through the bush to reach a destination.

There was one CA where we were being dropped in a mountainous area. Artillery had been working this area over, and there were a lot of broken and downed trees in the landing zone. To make things worse, we were landing on the side of a hill. Fortunately for me, my side of the helicopter was close to the ground. I stood on the skid until the pilot brought the chopper to a hover, then jumped from a couple of feet or so in height. Not so for the guys on the other side; they had quite the jump, with full gear. One of the guys impaled his leg on a broken sapling as he jumped, and had to be medevac'd for treatment. All in a day's work in 'Nam. It don't mean nothing....

On each CA outside of the Rice Bowl the gunships would 'fire up' the landing zone with the mini-gun and/or rockets before the choppers would drop us in. This would be done after artillery had already covered the area with a nice barrage. The purpose of this was to discourage any enemy in the area from taking a pot shot at us while we were coming in. Then, as we approached, our helicopter door gunners would open up on any suspicious cover in and around the LZ. On my first few CAs in this AO I wondered what in the world they were shooting at. I couldn't see anything. Then I began to learn they did it on every CA. One never wanted to land in a hot LZ. A hot LZ was a landing zone where the enemy was firing at the approaching grunts on the helicopters. Only once did we drop into what I would call a hot LZ; but this hot landing zone was not hot because of enemy fire. It was hot because we were being dropped into a meadow that had tall grass growing, and it was the dry season. The gunships firing in the LZ had set the grass on fire. As we approached on our choppers, I could see the smoke in the LZ from a distance and wondered what in the world we were getting into. Thankfully, that's all it was.

There was another kind of grass we had to contend with in the bush. That was elephant grass. This stuff was impossible. I don't know what the official name for this stuff was, but we ran into it from time to time. The idea was to avoid it. This stuff grew upwards of six feet tall. It was stiff, even thick, and the edges were razor sharp. If we ever had to cut trail thru the stuff, whoever was walking point that day and swinging the machete would probably need medical attention when we came out the other side. Rolling down the shirt sleeves was an absolute must when we couldn't avoid a patch.

The grass that burned in our "hot LZ" wasn't elephant grass, thank goodness. We disembarked from the choppers and formed a temporary perimeter, waiting for the choppers to clear out. Once it was quiet, we moved out from the LZ into the area that had been assigned for us to investigate on this mission. After some time, we took a break in a dried rice paddy that had a creek on one side and a terrace rising above it on the other side. Ken Cameron and another guy had gone down to the creek while the rest of us were taking a break. I was leaning against the rise of the terrace; others were perched atop the terrace. It was a nice quiet setting, a nice place to rest. One of the locals, however, decided to interrupt our rest and started shooting at us with sniper fire. I was always amazed at how fast I could get to the prone position when something happened. We were all down, but very exposed in the dried out rice paddy; everyone was looking for the sniper. Then...bang, bang. It was like slow motion; I still see it today. I saw two rounds hit the dry earth right in front of my head, not six inches away, just like in the movies. I am thankful the VC guy was a bad shot. Everybody was looking all over for the guy. We never saw him, but knew about where he was—and it was pretty close to us. During the ruckus, Ken and the other guy made a dash from the creek to our position. LT called in artillery on the sniper's suspected location. "Thump, thump, thump, thump…" The shot was out and on the way; then came the screech that got louder and louder, then detonation. The stuff landed so close, the ground we were clinging to shook, and we were covered with debris from the explosions. Fortunately, no one was hurt during any of this. We were just mad at the sniper. LT sent out a squad to patrol the area where the sniper was thought to have been, but nothing was found.

Later on that same mission, we were on a mountain looking across a valley and spotted an enemy location on the side of an adjacent mountain. There were bunkers and other structures that were clearly visible through the binoculars. LT called in an airstrike on it, and we had 'front row' seats as the spotter plane laid a couple of marking rockets on the location and the jet came in and dropped its ordinance. We were a good distance away, but the concussion from the bombs going off shook everything where we were. I would not have wanted to be on the receiving end of such a display. I was thankful we were not told to cross the valley below us and check out the location. It would have been a long walk down the mountain we were on, and the valley below was wide with only dried-out grass for cover. We would have been very exposed making that trek.

Returning to SJH after each mission was a real break in the action, allowing us down time to once again listen to music, send and receive mail, as well as have some hot food and a welcomed shower. It wasn't long after moving to this AO that I received a 35mm camera that I had ordered. The deals we got on things like cameras and stereo equipment were really good. I bought a full stereo system and had it shipped home; I had the camera shipped to me. Our cameras were kept secure in the company area at Bronco. Every time we came out of the bush I would request—ahead of time—that my camera be brought out to SJH from the rear. Several others did the same thing.

Left: Lonnie Johnson and Dale Hill in camera wars.
Right: Dale Hill demonstrating proper use of government issued shaving cream.

We had lots of fun taking pictures while learning how to operate our new cameras. Two of our guys, Dale Hill and Lonnie Johnson, were really good with the camera, and I remember how they helped the rest of us get comfortable with our new cameras. Dale was the technical type about the photography, while Lonnie was the artistic one. I always had a camera with me, even on missions in the bush, but I only took the 35mm on one mission. All other missions I carried a small instamatic camera wrapped in plastic, that fit perfectly in an ammo pouch I wore attached to my canteen belt. We would often swap cameras with each other, so our film could capture pictures of ourselves.

I still chuckle about one event that happened on San Juan Hill. I rank it up as another exposure to "military intelligence". Here I am, several months into my tour as a grunt in Vietnam. I am a draftee. If I had a choice, I would be at home. And what does the Army do? They try to talk me into signing up for more. I thought this was absolutely crazy! I was told a re-up guy was on the hill and wanted to talk to everyone. I think we had to go. I don't remember for sure, but it all seemed a joke to me. What's a guy to do? That's the Army way! So I go see the guy. He's in the mess hall. I am all ears as he gives me his pitch. What can you offer a guy who doesn't want to be here and has a job waiting for him back in the world? He didn't offer me anything that got my attention, that's for sure! Being a re-up guy must have been one tough job. I always wondered if he made his quota. Anyway, I gave one of my buddies my camera and asked him to take a picture of me getting the sales pitch. I looked 'really' interested. HA!

Talking to the re-up guy on SJH.

Our missions in the AO soon came to an end because of the upcoming Stand Down of the 4th of the 21st. A Stand Down was just that. The unit involved would 'stand down' from active involvement in action. Sometimes a Stand Down was just for a few days, to allow the troops to get away from the war and relax in the rear area. Other times, a Stand Down took place when a unit was being removed from service and made inactive. The upcoming Stand Down for the 4th/21st was the latter. 4th Platoon's (and Bravo Company's) last task on San Juan Hill was to 'remodel' it, so it could be turned over to the ARVN. We spent several days on SJH demolishing bunkers, fighting positions, and structures. Army engineers used a Sky Crane helicopter to fly out a bulldozer. They used the bulldozer to level the ground where all of these structures had been. At one point, after structures were demolished, the bulldozer was pushing and covering a debris field when it knocked a huge boulder loose from the ground. Down the hill it rolled until it was stopped by our squad's fighting position. Fortunately no one was home because we were all at "work".

Members of 4th Platoon relaxing with the boulder. (Dale Hill)

For the next few days we played hosts to the SJH boulder until the fighting positions were demolished and the rest of the hill was cleared off. When we left San Juan Hill, it was a small outpost on top of the highest point of the mountain that had housed men from the Americal Division for several years. The 1st Company, 2nd Battalion, 4th ARVN Regiment arrived on San Juan Hill and our time there came to an end. I always wondered what happened to San Juan Hill after we left.

We returned to Duc Pho and to Stand Down. All of the men who had fewer than 90 days left on their tour in Vietnam were given early drops and orders to return home. Many of the men I had come to know and trust had made it. Dale Hill, Michael Gatewood, David Myers, and some others were going home! I was not. Dale Doege, Tom Duran and I received orders to join 4th Battalion 3rd Infantry Regiment in Chu Lai. When we got there, we met others who had been a part of Bravo Company (in other platoons)—Charlie Dault (from CP Platoon) and Larce Kyzer (from 1st Platoon). We were all assigned to the first platoon at our new unit—Delta Company. I was still in my tunnel, but was there light at the other end? For the first time, I was seeing an end to my tour. It was still a long way off, but I had just seen some of my buddies head home. I was happy for them, and it gave me hope to see them make it. Maybe I would too!

All that was left of San Juan Hill after the 'remodel job' done by Bravo Company.

DELTA 4/3 AND LZ PROFESSIONAL

This unit was different. The Area of Operations (AO) was different. Life was different. Everything was different. I don't know why. Maybe it was me. I had been in country six months now. I was halfway through my tunnel. I have fewer memories from the months spent with the 4th/3rd than the months spent with the 4th/21st. I have no explanation for that. With 4th Platoon, today I remember names and faces of those I was with. With the 4th/3rd unit, the only people I remember are those that came with me from Bravo Company—Dale, Tom, Charlie, and Larce. I do remember some specific events, as if seared into my memory and, thanks to the daily TOC reports I received, have been able to piece together even more. One thing I clearly remember is that we worked in very small groups—eight to twelve men most of the time, almost like a Recon Team. As I recalled this, it seemed to me that the platoon I was in must have been very understrength; but the TOC reports explained this. Each night all battalion units would radio their location to the Tactical Operation Center (TOC). This was done so all artillery and other support units would know where all the friendlies were. The daily logs showed a specific map coordinate for each squad for each platoon. This means that, instead of working in platoon-sized elements, we were working in squad-size. Most logs only showed two squads per platoon; thus, we were probably understrength because a platoon usually has four squads. Another thing the

4th/3rd did that was new to me was we conducted Eagle Flights—lots of Eagle Flights… more on this later. The AO had much more enemy activity, and the new unit was much more aggressive in their pursuit of the enemy than Bravo Company had been.

Left to Right: Charlie Dault, Dale Doege, Larce Kyzar and me at the South China Sea beach in Chu Lai during a Stand Down.

The rear area for the 4th/3rd was in Chu Lai; that is where we reported upon our arrival, after leaving 4th/21st in Duc Pho. Soon we were on a chopper to the LZ our company worked off. It was LZ Professional; and it was approximately 20 miles northwest of Chu Lai—a long way from anywhere, compared to what I had been exposed to so far.

Pro was a small mountain in the center of a valley, but to its south were higher mountains. I never understood that. Why would we not be on the tallest mountain in the area? My fighting position on the LZ perimeter, when in from the bush, was on the south side of the LZ, and I would sit and stare at that big mountain and wonder if someone was looking down at me. There was at least one time when something was going on over there, because I remember watching a "Flame Drop". A flame drop involved a Chinook helicopter hovering over an area, dropping containers of fuel. Then a gunship, accompanying the Chinook, would light it on fire with machine gun fire. On this particular occasion, they were flaming a bunker complex that had been spotted by one of the helicopters that was in and out of LZ Pro all the time. The Chinook dropped all sorts of fuel on the area. It must have been in the thousands of gallons. When the gunship fired it up, it made quite a fire. I was really glad someone spotted those bunkers, because if someone had been using them they would have been looking right at me. Who knows how old they were, or whether there had even been recent activity there...I was just glad they were spotted and dealt with. They had the high ground, and everyone on the south side of Pro would have been a sitting duck.

105mm howitzer, like the one behind my bunker on Pro.

Also, just above and behind our fighting position on LZ Pro was an artillery pit that housed a 105mm howitzer. We didn't do much sleeping when they were busy supporting guys in the field. They would always be firing right over our heads. When they had a fire mission (artillery shooting) everything shook, including me. Can anyone say, "Are your ears ringing, too?" Crazy...

Some guys called our fighting positions on Pro 'bunkers', but they were hardly that. A bunker had room for a few guys to sleep while someone was maintaining watch. This was not the case on Pro. Our positions were spaced along the perimeter, connected to each other by a sandbagged trench. The position consisted of half a metal culvert piece placed on top of a stack of wooden ammo crates filled with dirt. The whole structure would then be covered with sandbags. The front of the fighting position would also be built up with boxes and sandbags to offer protection from those bad guys outside the perimeter. These were strictly fighting positions with no room for sleeping. Sleeping was done on the ground or on top of the position. The only time I slept in the position was when it was raining—and the mosquitos inside these things were unbearable.

Me sleeping atop fighting position on Professional.

The helicopter unit that worked in this AO would conduct Night Hawk flights, which would have choppers out looking for enemy activity in his domain—the night. These guys could bring a 'real hurt' to the enemy. Night Hawk could be composed of several helicopters of different capabilities, but the Bell UH-1 helicopter (known as the Huey), that was the primary one, carried a very powerful starlight scope (night vision), large spotlight, and armaments of the mini-gun (4,000 rounds per minute) and 40mm grenade launcher. If these guys spotted the enemy they were very capable of firing them up while on station. I watched this happen one night and was impressed with the delivery of their munitions. Whenever these guys would have an encounter, or find a suspicious area like hooches, cultivated fields (that shouldn't have been there), or well-defined trails—the grids would be reported and an Eagle Flight would be called for.

We normally worked in squad-size elements; but an Eagle Flight involved a larger group. Often on these Eagle Flights, we would be CA'd to an area because there were reports of heavy enemy activity. Once we arrived, we would sweep the area, prepared to confront the enemy if present. We captured a lot of weapons, food, and other supplies on these missions, but never ran into any bad guys. That doesn't mean they weren't around; it was clear to us they were around.

On my first Eagle Flight we were dropped off in a large meadow and then moved on line across the meadow into the wood line beyond it. We were fully exposed, so I was glad to reach the trees. Once in the woods, however, we discovered a large area that was being used as some sort of staging area.

Campfires were still burning, food was in the pots, chickens were running around, papers were lying around, and there were a lot of hooches—about 15 or 20. Some of these hooches had bunkers or tunnels under them. Apparently the sound of approaching helicopters had given the residents the opportunity to evade into the jungle or into their tunnels before our arrival. In their haste they had left a lot of stuff lying around. Dale Doege saw an M-1 carbine in one of the tunnels. He considered grabbing it, but decided to leave it in the dark tunnel entrance because he couldn't check it thoroughly enough without exposing himself in a vulnerable way. As we swept through the area, I spotted a Chinese SKS rifle leaning against a tree. I was checking it out, to be sure it wasn't booby trapped, when another guy (I never knew who he was) came running up and grabbed it. He claimed his war trophy, and I was really mad that he was so reckless. Thankfully the rifle wasn't rigged to anything and we walked away. After we checked out the entire area, the choppers returned and we were pulled out. No one ever went into any of the tunnels, and we didn't destroy anything there. We just left. Usually when we discovered these types of places we would destroy the hooches along with food that might have been discovered. Tunnels and bunkers would also be destroyed. Weapons and munitions would be hauled back to LZ Pro or Chu Lai. I didn't understand why we just left this location, and I never knew what the final result was for all of this effort, but the enemy had a really nice spot there in the woods. We never saw a single person, but I always had the bad feeling they were watching us. Spooky...

A typical CA pickup using a large number of choppers.

We conducted many Eagle Flights over the next few months, but they were done while on our normal missions. Our normal missions with this new unit had some similarities to the missions we ran off San Juan Hill back at 4th/21st, only in this AO the locals were much less sociable. These guys were the North Vietnamese Army (NVA), or some of the locals who supported them. We would still stay out 12 days, and then rotate back to the hill for four days, while being resupplied every three days. Then we'd do it all again. These guys, however, spent a lot of time walking on some very well-used trails. A well-used trail could only mean one thing—there were others out there doing a lot of walking on those trails, too. I sure hoped we never bumped into any of them. Whenever we stopped to take a break in this AO, we made sure to set out a mech on any trail we had been walking or observing. It was just standard procedure here. On one occasion, we had been walking a well-used trail and pulled off to take a break. We moved well off the trail without leaving any sign of our presence. Then a couple of the guys went back and set up a mech and then returned to our lunch spot. As we were sitting eating lunch...bang! The mech detonated. A small group of us quickly moved to the area and found nothing—no blood, no bodies—nothing. This really put us on edge. It could have been the wind or an animal that set it off, but now our presence was made known. That was not good. We quickly gathered our stuff and continued on our mission, now more alert than ever. Finding nothing in a blown mech was not the usual discovery. Another day, again while eating lunch and resting, we had set a mech on the trail we had left. When it detonated, a group of us approached the area and discovered a single NVA soldier had been killed. There was no sign of another enemy around. The guy was fully loaded with over 200 rounds of AK-47 ammo, along with his AK-47 rifle, and a diary. A diary, or other documents, is the kind of stuff the military intelligence people loved to get their hands on. The military intelligence groups would provide reports of their discoveries to the units working in the field. There was lots of intel at this time that showed several different units of NVA and VC were operating in our AO. This intel came from live sources and also from captured documents. While we were checking this NVA guy's stuff, two more NVA came walking up the trail. They were fully armed (often we would spot enemy who were not armed, or only some would be armed) and spotted us just before we spotted them. Rather than engage us, they took off in the opposite direction. We were fortunate they decided to di-di (get out of there) rather than fire us up. We were more in number, but they had the drop on us. It could have been a bad moment. We fired in their direction, but they were gone in no time. There was no sign that we had inflicted a wound on them. We radioed in for a Dog Team to be sent out to help us track them. Meanwhile, we buried the enemy KIA in a shallow grave.

Such was life in the new AO. There were lots of bad guys running around, and this kept me pretty much on edge all the time. The only relatively safe place here was when we were on LZ Pro. There was no "front line" anywhere. We never knew if, when we turned the next corner on a trail, there would be a group of NVA coming in our direction. We never knew whether they might have heard us approaching and gone into a quick ambush. "It don't mean nothing" morphed from an attitude of "it's no big deal" to the thought of "I could die around the next turn." I didn't dwell on it, but that was the reality.

BECOMING A MACHINE GUNNER

It was about this time that one of the platoon's M-60 gunners was rotating out to go home. I volunteered to become the new gunner so I wouldn't have to walk point any more. I didn't like these trails, or the folks that used them. I liked them even less when I was the point man. So I began my new job as the M-60 gunner. One of the other gunners got me squared away with the M-60 while we were on LZ Professional. I fired off a bunch of rounds at the make-shift range we had; disassembled it; cleaned it; and got it all back together without leaving anything out. I tried firing the M-60 from different positions to get used to the feel of it. My most comfortable firing position was kneeling with my left hand holding the gun and my left elbow resting on my left leg; the stock of the gun was under my right arm, with my right hand on the pistol grip/trigger area. I could easily self-feed the ammo belt as it moved across my left arm into the gun.

The M-60 machine gun weighed in at 24 pounds (compared to six pounds for the M-16). The ammunition for the M-60 was a belt of cartridges instead of a magazine like the M-16. A full M-60 team consisted of three men—the gunner, the assistant gunner (AG), and the ammo bearer. The AG would help feed the ammo when the gun was firing and would also help spot targets. The ammo bearer did exactly what the name implied; he carried lots of extra ammo. That was the official Army description of the M-60 machine gun crew. Reality, though, was often different from official designs; such was the case with us. I was the gunner and Dale was the AG, but all that meant was he carried more ammo than the rest of the guys in the platoon and walked next to me when we were on the move. Everyone else in the platoon carried 100 rounds of M-60 ammo. The M-60 ammo had a tracer round every fifth round in the belt. This round was visible when shot and helped in placing the fire onto a target. The tracer round also made the M-60 quite visible, day or night, but especially at night. M-60 gunners were often targeted by the enemy because of this. I understood this risk and considered walking point more risky. I used a heavy canvas sling around my neck, hooked to either end of the gun to help carry it. This helped a lot when I needed both hands to grab stuff while pulling up a hill in the jungle. This carrying style also gave me quick access to the gun as it lay across my chest. I would carry a few hundred rounds of ammo on my pack and around my waist, with another 50 or so connected to the gun, ready to fire if needed. Fortunately, I only had to use the gun once in the field in an active combat situation.

This is me all loaded up and ready to leave LZ Professional on another mission.

Well, that's sort of true…there was one time where several of us were on a patrol and one of the guys said he spotted some enemy guys about 200 yards away, across a bombed out area in the jungle. We were in a tree line, looking across this wide area of downed trees and debris into another tree line. We had good cover and everyone took a position. I found a spot behind a large log, allowing me to prop the M-60 on top of it. The others joined me in this spot. I'm looking for the enemy and can't see anybody out there. Some of the other guys also saw nothing. We look to the guy who spotted them and whispered, "Where?" He looked for a minute and then said they were there, next to a big tree. I still didn't see anybody. He clarified which tree it was and said they were just to the left of it. I saw nothing. Everybody is ready to open up and tell me to fire first—at nothing… I say ok, flick off the safety on the M-60 and pull the trigger. BANG! One shot! I look, and everybody is looking at me with a 'what the hell?' face on! What's a guy to do? I pulled back the bolt, seated another round, and pulled the trigger. I repeated this action several times as the other guys shot their M-16s. There I was, the proud operator of a single shot, bolt action M-60 machine gun. The gun was supposed to fire in the neighborhood of 500-600 rounds per minute. My firing rate was a little below that. The gun was a gas-operated weapon, which meant the air pressure and gases released from firing one round would be used to activate the bolt action of ejecting the spent cartridge and seating the next round in the chamber. There was a cylinder on the gun that was pressurized during firing. What had happened in this case was the cylinder had a leak because I had not properly seated the locking bolt on the cylinder when I last cleaned the weapon. This was a really serious oversight on my part that could have put me and those around me in a very precarious position. We were very fortunate that day this was not the case. When we returned from our patrol, I disassemble the gun for cleaning, re-assembled it, and asked the LT if I could test fire it. With a look of, "you better have it right" he told me to go ahead. Everything worked fine. I had learned a really important lesson—always double-check assembly; always test fire the weapon.

The more serious incident occurred a few weeks later. We were again working along some well-used trails in the mountains and pulled off the trail a good distance to set up a night perimeter. A couple of guys returned to the trail to set up a mech. The location was perfect for concealing the devices, and the trail was obviously well traveled. The guys used detonating cord (det cord) to string multiple claymores together. The night passed without incident. But in the morning, rather than retrieving the mech and moving on, our LT decided we would patrol the area and move our perimeter to the other side of the trail at the end of the day, leaving the mech in place all day and the next night. Late that day, after we had moved to our new night perimeter on top of a small hill, the mech detonated. Larce, our squad leader, quickly led a few of us down the hill, up a creek and near to the mech site. We didn't know what lay ahead for us and our senses were all on edge. On top of that, it was almost dark. We approached, using the creek to cover any noise we might be making, and Larce asked me to cover the area with M-60 fire before we moved in to investigate. I quickly fired off about 150 rounds in 10-15 round bursts along the route of the trail before we approached. Then the M-60 jammed. I attempted to clear the gun, but a round was locked sideways in the chamber. There was a lever on the M-60 machine gun that allowed for a quick release of the barrel. I flipped the lever and dumped the barrel out of the body of the gun. I was standing in a creek and the end of the barrel landed in the water, sizzling in the coolness of the water. I saw the cross-fed round in the back end of the barrel; when I attempted to grab it (not a smart move), my finger got burned pretty badly. So I dumped the entire barrel into the water, retrieved it, and then pulled the round out. I re-seated the barrel in the gun, chambered a round, and told Larce I was ready to do some more. He said I had done enough, and we moved forward to inspect the mech area. When we approached, we found four NVA soldiers—killed from the mech, the M-60, or both. It was not a pretty sight. One of them was a paymaster or something, as he was carrying a lot of money. We never met the guys he was planning on paying...thankfully. Our small group formed a rough perimeter as Larce checked out the results of our work. Then, all of a sudden...crash! Anyone who was standing dropped quickly for cover. Everybody was tense, but it turned out to be nothing. A small tree fell over, scaring all of us like crazy. I had 'chopped' down the tree with the shooting of the M-60, but the tree waited until we were close by before it fell. We quickly policed up the money, some documents and a couple of weapons and ammo, and returned to our perimeter. We stayed on edge for a while after that. We didn't know if the guys we killed were headed to a place close to where we were, but knew that was a very real possibility. In the middle of the night, gunshots awoke those of us who had finally fallen off to sleep. I rolled out of my hammock onto the ground where the M-60 lay, waiting for use. It was totally dark, and now totally quiet—no jungle noises, nothing, just absolute silence. Nobody knew what was going on. Larce then crawled around our squad's area of the perimeter to tell us that one of the guys shot at what must have been a wild boar, or some other animal that was making noise in front of his position. He had been a bit edgy with the rest of us, and now we were all the more wired up. We slept very little the rest of that night. The next morning a resupply chopper brought us fresh ammo and claymores, along with a dog team for tracking the trail of any enemy that might have escaped the mech the night before. The handler and his dog stayed with us until the next regular re-supply. There was no more action on this mission that I remember.

Darkness in the bush required absolute noise and light discipline. There could be no varying this. Mistakes sent people home in body bags. One of our new guys learned the importance of light discipline on his first night in the bush. We received a couple of new guys on a resupply chopper and that night we were setting up our night positions. It had gotten dark enough to just see the shapes of the other men close by. Total darkness had not yet arrived. One of the new guys decided it was time for a smoke. Out came his cigarette lighter and, with a flick of his finger, he had a nice flame going in his hand. The entire perimeter was lit up. Before he could get that flame to the end of his cigarette, three guys were on top of him snuffing out the lighter's flame. Since the new guy needed a smoke, the next step was to show him how to smoke at night without revealing your location. I was a smoker at the time and prided myself in being able to burn one without being seen in the black dark. The smallest light could be seen from a great distance in the darkness—so great care had to be taken in this endeavor. The process was this: I began underneath my poncho liner; then I would pull my night shirt (a long-sleeved pullover shirt we wore at night) over my head; I would then bend over, next to the ground; then I would bring my hands up inside my shirt and cup my hands around the end of the cigarette while holding it between my lips. The lighter would then be flicked on for as short a time as possible, and that first pleasurable draw taken from the smoke that was cupped protectively in my hands. Smoke would be exhaled inside the shirt to minimize the smell drifting away, giving our enemy an alert. Further draws on the cigarette would all be done in the same manner until the smoke was complete. The smoke would be extinguished by lowering it to the ground and pushing it into the ground, breaking it into small, undetectable pieces.

THE MAN I KILLED

Life for the grunt seemed to be an endless list of 12-day missions all lined up waiting to be checked off. Each of these missions offered the same thing to us grunts—the unknown. We never knew what we would face as we loaded up to begin a new mission. Would it be quiet? Would we hit some bad stuff? Would someone get hurt or killed? We didn't talk about these things, but they were always in our minds. We took the "It don't mean nothing" attitude and moved ahead. On one of these many missions, we had been out for several days and all had been quiet. We were taking a break, and Larce asked me, Charlie Dault, and one other guy to go on a patrol. On a small patrol like this, I would leave the M-60 behind and grab someone's M-16 and ammo. On this occasion, I borrowed the medic's M-16 without checking it out thoroughly. I didn't know that our medic didn't keep a round in the chamber of his M-16 like everyone else did. With a round in the chamber, all one had to do to fire was flip the safety off and pull the trigger; but with no round in the chamber, one had to pull back the bolt, release it to chamber a round, then release the safety and pull the trigger. So, here I was walking point on a three-man patrol, without knowing there was no round in the chamber of the M-16 I carried. We hadn't gone far, and had just entered a creek bed, when my slack man tapped me on the shoulder and pointed down the creek. There was a VC guy cleaning something at the creek's edge. We quickly dropped behind a boulder, thankful that the noise of the creek had kept any noise we might have made from being heard the few

126

yards away by the VC. We decided to quietly move out of the creek and return to the platoon rather than engage him at that moment. There were just three of us. We were in the middle of nowhere and thought it very unusual to bump into a single VC. The chance of others being around was really good, though we hadn't seen anyone else. We slipped out of the creek and made the short trip back to the platoon to advise them of our find. LT got everyone up except for a couple of guys to stay with our stuff. He put me on point, since I had been on point going in initially; he told me when we got back to the site I would initiate firing. I still had Doc's M-16 and one of the other guys had the M-60. We made it back to the creek in short order; a couple of us slipped back down into the creek and got behind the same boulder I was behind before. The rest of the guys held back on the edge of the creek to avoid making too much noise. I eased up over the boulder and the guy was still there; still working on whatever he was working on. I eased the M-16 up, placed my sight on the guy, flipped off the safety, and pulled the trigger...click...oh shit! This 'moment' led to a series of events that still vividly live in my head today. I slowly pulled back on the bolt as quietly as I could; then, rather than releasing it, I quietly slid it forward to chamber a round. Again, I placed my sights on the man in front of me. Then things changed...I don't know what prompted his action, but at this very moment, the man in front of me stopped what he was doing and looked up—right at me—right into my eyes... Then I shot him. This action startled a second VC that we hadn't even seen. He jumped up and began to run away. The rest of our platoon rushed into the creek bed and began to fire at him, but everyone missed. One of our guys had the M-79 grenade launcher (blooper) and raised it to fire in the VC's direction as he was running away. The round hit a small branch of a tree above and in front of us, and detonated prematurely, scattering shrapnel over our area. We all moved forward to where the body of the enemy soldier lay, and then on up the trail where the other VC had evaded. We discovered a couple of new hooches, several hundred pounds of harvested food, some uniforms, medical supplies, hammocks, and documents. There were also a couple of heavily used trails in the area, meaning lots of bad guys were through this area all the time. The two VC we had discovered were living in an area that put them in harm's way, and they were obviously part of something bigger than just two guys living in the woods.

As things settled down a bit, someone looked at Charlie and said, "Hey, you are bleeding." Charlie had not realized he had been hit in the heat of the moment by some of the blooper shrapnel, and had blood running down his arm. Doc began to check him out and patch him up right away; the RTO (radio guy) called for a Dust-Off. The Dust-off was a medevac helicopter that transported wounded from the field to hospitals in the rear. While Doc was working on Charlie and the RTO was working on the Dust-Off, some of us were given another task. LT had us gather rocks from the creek to cover the body of the VC in a form of burial. As we did this, I got a close look at the results of my work. I had shot this man, whose now lifeless body lay next to the creek. I didn't think twice about it at the time. "It don't mean nothing" was the usual thought...but over the years this event has always been there as a reminder of the cost in war...to the dead and the survivors. This was different than firing up the NVA who had been caught in our mech on a previous mission. That firing had been done in a general direction and visibility had been way down because of the time of day. This was done in broad daylight, with full view of the enemy soldier, who was less than 100 feet away. This man had looked me in the eye; and I had shot him. This was really personal. He was where he shouldn't have been—according to our rules, but he was where he should have been—according to his rules. Maybe he was doing what he believed in that day. I was just there, doing what I was told; trying to make it to the end of my tour; not wanting to be there in the first place. What a screwed-up world! That man died that day, but he still lives with me, in my memories. "It don't mean nothing." Really?

As the Dust-off approached we heard the familiar thump, thump, thump of the helicopter blades beating against the air. There were two choppers coming in. The first on station was a Cobra Gunship. It flew directly over us and began to circle. The Cobras were sweet ships and could bring a lot of hurt to the enemy with the rockets and mini-gun they were armed with. I was always amazed at how the choppers were able to find us in the jungle, but find us they did—and without GPS that soldiers use today. There was a lot of radio talk between the Cobra and our RTO, and I'm sure this brought him right to us, along with the map coordinates that had been given on the initial Dust-Off call. The gunships, either Cobras or Hueys armed with rockets and door mounted, manually operated mini-guns, usually accompanied the medevacs when there had been contact with the enemy. The medevacs were also Huey helicopters; were unarmed; and were marked with a red cross emblem on the bottom and sides, clearly identifying them as a medical vehicle. We were told to pop smoke, and then the pilot identified our smoke color. We always waited for the pilot to identify the color of our smoke. Sometimes the VC would have smoke. If we broadcast the color of our smoke, and the VC were monitoring our radio frequency, they could pop the same color, and then fire up the chopper as it landed in their smoke. The medevac came in and hovered over our position. They then dropped a jungle penetrator through the jungle covering to our location. A jungle penetrator was a device that was lowered from the medevac helicopter by a metal cable. It was a slender contraption that could easily slip past tree branches. Once it was down, the penetrator could be opened into what looked something like an anchor. The injured soldier would sit on the arms of the penetrator and be hoisted up. This was a tricky operation that had to be done with great care. If a soldier was unable to sit, then the medevac would lower a basket for him to be placed in. Our medic got Charlie all hooked up on the penetrator and up he went, through the trees, being pulled safely into the medevac. Then he was off to Chu Lai for treatment.

I was credited with the enemy KIA (killed in action) and was granted a three-day R&R for my efforts. I learned that our battalion commander had recently announced this incentive program to jack up his enemy body count. I guess in his mind we weren't being aggressive enough. In Vietnam, it wasn't about taking ground and holding it; it was all about the body count. The body count was a measurement of success for field commanders, and the body count in 1971 was a lot lower than in previous years. Of course, for us grunts in the field, a low body count was a good thing. I don't know what gave the commander the idea of this three-day R&R incentive program; maybe he was looking to enhance his resume, or maybe higher-higher was on his back for not doing enough; but I ended up being a beneficiary of the program. The more people were pushed to raise the body count, the more chances commanders took with their men. The more chances taken by the commanders meant a greater risk of our guys being wounded or killed. This made me appreciate the leaders of 4th Platoon of Bravo Company, my previous unit, all the more.

I enjoyed my three days out of the bush. I went out on the next resupply chopper and was flown back to Chu Lai, the company and battalion rear area. A lot of guys took R&Rs during their tour by traveling to out-of-country destinations like Thailand, Australia, or Hawaii. This in-country R&R was the only one I took during my tour. I had no desire to travel to some exotic destination without Becki, and there was no way we could afford to fly her over to join me. I was sending most of my Army paycheck home every month already, and there wasn't much left to set up a fancy trip. So I settled in for three days in Chu Lai. I thoroughly enjoyed it. I popped a few tops in the NCO club every night, spent time at the South China Sea beach, visited the PX, ate three meals a day, and slept in a bed with sheets. I had no responsibilities more than getting up in time for breakfast if I wanted to eat it. It was a good three days. The only problem was that it just lasted three days. Then I was back on a chopper headed to LZ Professional to rejoin Delta Company who had come out of the bush at the end of their mission.

I remember once, on LZ Pro, someone showed up with a Tommy gun. We were all fascinated with it. We took it to the back of the hill to our range and fired off some rounds. I got a turn and really liked it, though it packed a punch and was difficult to hold steady. I also spent some extra time on LZ Pro, missing one of our missions. I had developed what we called gook sores on my legs that got pretty nasty, and the medic got me out of the bush to let my legs heal up. The sores developed from a combination of heat, water, dirt, and rubbing from clothing or boots; and they were pretty painful when they got out of hand. Mine hurt a good bit. The cure beyond ointment was dryness and air. This would have been impossible to obtain in the bush, so I got a few days of rest on Pro.

There was another mission where we discovered a large, abandoned enemy base camp. It looked like it hadn't been used for a few months, but it was full of bunkers and other structures, and could easily have been put back into service. It was decided to request that some engineers come out and demolish the camp. This was an interesting experience. We had to wait around for a while before the explosive guys showed up, but when their chopper arrived I was impressed. They (we) off-loaded a variety of explosive devices. Some were designed to be placed into bunkers and cause a collapse and others were shaped to bring down trees that provided good cover for the camp. I watched as these guys did their work, strategically placing their charges and connecting everything with det cord. I got a pound of C-4 from one of the guys and told him I was going to knock over a small tree (about two-three inches in diameter). The pound of C-4 had double-sided tape on one side of it, so I removed the tape cover and wrapped my "explosive charge" around the little tree. Then got some det cord and connected it to the det cord that was running all through the camp. The guy that had given me the C-4 had been watching me do all this and had an expression on his face like, "...this dummy...what's he think he's doing...?" Well, I was all set! Once the engineers had set all of their devices, we all cleared the area and they detonated their charges with one big BOOM! After the dust cleared we returned to the area. What a job they had done. The bunkers were a total mess and the large trees had been toppled; however, my little tree was still standing. A ring of bark was missing where the C-4 had been placed. Thus I had a very practical lesson in the advantage of using shaped and directional charges.

And so it went...12 days in the bush and four days on the hill; then wind it up and do it all over again. Each mission was unique because I never knew what I might face, and each mission was the same—danger, heat, exhaustion, mosquitos, and more danger. We never had any large scale face-to-face battles, or even skirmishes. It was always hit and run—and it was us doing the hitting and them doing the running, if they could. Rarely did we see the enemy before a mech detonated; but almost every day we saw signs of the enemy—fresh signs. Maybe it was a fresh footprint on a trail; maybe a warm cooking location; or a hooch recently used—the signs were all around us, and it kept us on edge all day and all night for each 12-day mission.

The C-130

One of my last missions in the field once again provided me with a unique experience. The mission started as all other missions had started. We were all geared up and ready to go from the helicopter pad on Pro. Each platoon was picked up and CA'd to their designated area for the mission. After a few days during this mission, we were told to proceed to an LZ for pickup. Often, when working in the mountains and jungles of Vietnam, finding a good LZ was a challenge. There just weren't a lot of places to land a helicopter for pickup, so some serious planning had to go into finding a good one for resupply and end-of-mission pickup. When a call came to move to an LZ for pickup, we first had to find one. This took some doing, but after some patrolling we located a clearing large enough and called in the coordinates. Then it was just a matter of waiting for the choppers. It wasn't long before we heard that familiar thump, thump, thump of the approaching helicopters. We popped smoke and in they came. We were lifted to an area to join the rest of Delta Company. Once the entire company had arrived, we heard an approaching aircraft. Making a turn in the distance was a C-130 cargo plane. I'm thinking, "Surely this guy is not coming for us!" But, in he came and dropped right down on the airstrip at our location, rolled in our direction, turned around, and dropped his cargo door. That's when the orders came for us to climb on board. I had flown on a C-130 one other time, on my arrival in Vietnam, 10 months earlier, when I flew from Cam Ranh Bay to Chu Lai. I had been seated in a canvas seat along the inner wall of the airplane. I knew from that experience that there was no way our entire company of fully loaded grunts was going to fit inside that airplane. When I got to the ramp, I noticed there were no seats. The first guys in were told to walk to the front of the cargo bay, turn around, sit on the floor, and lean against the front bulkhead. Then they were to bend their knees and pull their legs up against their chest. The next group of guys was to follow the same procedure, except they were to lean against the legs of the guys who just sat down. The airplane's loadmaster made sure every one of us got squeezed into that C-130. I now knew what a sardine felt like. One thing was for sure...no one was going to be sliding around.

Having ridden in a C-130 before, I thought I knew what to expect, even though I wasn't in the nice comfy canvas seat along the side of the airplane. Oh boy was I mistaken! The loadmaster raised the door at the back of the cargo bay, and the pilot started revving up the engines. It was loud beyond belief, and the airplane was shaking like it was going to fall apart at any minute. It had been 10 months since I rode that C-130 from Cam Ranh Bay to Chu Lai—this ride was nothing like that ride. Maybe this C-130 was a bit 'older' than the one I rode before, I don't know. I just didn't remember all the noise and shaking from that first trip. And, as a grunt, I'm used to riding with my face in the wind and legs hanging out the door of a chopper. Here I'm cooped up inside an airplane that sounds and feels like it is getting ready to disintegrate. I'm getting a bit nervous, and the facial and verbal expressions from those around me echoed how I felt. Not a soul near me had any confidence in what we were about to do. We all felt the airplane begin to roll, and all I could see in my imagination was what we were going to look like splashed all over the runway. Louder and louder! Shakier and shakier! Down the airstrip we went, picking up speed. Everyone got really quiet...we might have been holding our collective breath! Another few seconds of this and either we would hit the trees and the plane would disintegrate into a billion pieces of airplane parts and grunts' body parts, or we would be airborne. Then, we felt that unmistakable smoothness of rising off the ground. After a few more seconds I knew we had to have cleared the trees, and I relaxed some. It was still unbelievably loud and the airplane was still shaking violently, but we were flying. The only problem was...we still had to land.

I was glad I didn't have to watch us land. The strip we landed on was a small strip at a firebase called Tien Phuoc (pronounced tin fook). We disembarked and got a glimpse of our new location, still not knowing why we were there. Tien Phuoc had a long history with the American and South Vietnamese military. It was created as a Special Forces camp early in the Vietnam War. At that time, it had a dirt airstrip that could accommodate a C-123 cargo airplane. Because of its location, it had been in the crosshairs of the NVA for a long time. It had even been under siege in the late 1960s by the NVA. The Americal Division, elements of the 101st Airborne Division, and all available air support at the time had been tasked with coming to the aid of the base while it was under siege. They had fought long and hard, with many casualties, to reach the area and drive the NVA out. Over the years the firebase had grown from a Special Forces camp, with one artillery battery, to a large base that housed several artillery batteries. I remember several very large artillery pieces at this location. I know at one point during the war there were 105mm howitzers, 155s, 175s and eight-inch guns. This was really big stuff. Whether all of these artillery pieces were present at this time I am not sure, but they did have more than just the 105. I was familiar with the 105s on Pro, but these were pieces I had never seen before. Because of all of the growth that had taken place over the years, the small dirt runway had been upgraded to a steel mesh-surfaced runway long enough to accommodate a C-130; that is how they were able to receive our flight. So here we were. We soon learned that we were going to pull perimeter security for one of the artillery batteries during the night. A group of them was pulling out in the morning, and we would join the convoy as a security force for them as they withdrew to the rear for stand down. These guys were going home! They must have been excited... I was envious...

We were assigned our bunkers for the night and got settled in. The bunker I was assigned was in pretty bad shape structurally, and it wasn't clean. Whoever had been here had not taken care of the place; but I knew it was just for one night and then I'd be out of there. What the heck. "It don't mean nothing". I joined the other two men who were assigned the same bunker; we laid out our stuff and decided how to divide the security responsibilities. Then we cooked up come C-Rations. Dark didn't come as early here because there were no trees over us, but the darkness did come. Night in Vietnam, and one hopes it stays quiet. It didn't. All was well around the perimeter, but the arty guys got some calls for fire missions, and they started firing their big guns. Man! Everything shook. The ground shook, the bunker shook, and I shook. I would not have wanted to have been on the receiving end of whatever it was they were sending down range. They didn't fire long; then all was quiet. They had one more fire mission during the night, but that was it.

In the morning we were up and getting ready to roll out. C-Rations were eaten and coffee was drunk. Gear was packed up; then we waited. The arty guys had to load up a bunch of stuff and break down their gear. Once they were ready, we were loaded into duce-and-a-half trucks and mixed in with the convoy. We were to be a quick reaction force if the convoy was hit. It was a quiet ride through the country and we all reached their destination, Tam Ky, safely. We left the arty guys in Tam Ky and proceeded on to Chu Lai where we were taken to a tarmac and once again boarded helicopters and returned to the bush to finish our mission.

THE REAR AND GOING HOME

As the summer passed, I was getting short (i.e., getting close to going home) and was really hoping some rumors going around about another Stand Down would come true. Rumors, though, are just that; and the Army was full of them. With the approach of October, however, I was notified by the company First Sergeant that I had been selected for a job in the rear area, working in supply. I was ecstatic. I couldn't believe it! There really was light at the end of my tunnel! I was not going back to the bush! When the company left Pro to begin their next mission, I would be going to Chu Lai. I quickly announced the news in letters home to the family. This was the best news I had received from the Army since being drafted over a year before. I owed Tom Duran a big thanks for this selection. Shortly after we had arrived at Delta Company Tom had been given a job in the rear working as a clerk. It was Tom's suggestion that had won me the spot in supply.

Well, my ride to the rear actually came before the company left for their mission. When the chopper was ready to go, some of the guys from my platoon spoke to the pilot and told him the ride was my short-timer's ride (last helicopter ride in the bush). He turned and looked at me as I was sitting with my feet dangling out the side of the chopper. He grinned, gave me a thumbs up, and off we went...right down the side of the hill and across the valley just above the grass blowing in the helicopter's rotor downwash. This guy was flying fast and low, to give me one last rush on my last chopper ride! I had the wind in my face and was grinning ear to ear. I could see home on the other side of Chu Lai! He soon pulled up to a cruising altitude and off we went to my destination. It was September 25th, and the bush was behind me. I had made it!

Working in supply in the rear area was quite a change from the 12-day missions I was used to. I had three hot meals a day, went to work after breakfast, and got off work just before supper... and I'm really stretching it to call it work. I shared the eight-hour day with two other guys. We had to keep an inventory of stuff to meet the needs of the grunts in the field and keep records for whatever came in and went out. That was it. I spent a lot of time writing letters home, reading, and listening to music. There was a lot of time to visit the Chu Lai PX (Military Wal-Mart), go to the beach, and get a burger at the local hang-out by the PX. Life was good. The nights were pleasant too. I had bunker security occasionally, but not that often, and I slept in a bed with a mattress and sheets; and I showered every day. It was like taking in a long deep breath and just letting it go, nice and slow...wonderful...relaxing!

The light at the end of my tunnel was getting brighter each and every day. I was thinking about home and watching the days go by, knowing that home was closer and closer. Two big events occurred during my last weeks in Vietnam in Chu Lai— one was the USO show with Miss America and her traveling friends that I got to attend, and the other was typhoon Hester that I also attended.

USO show with Miss America in Chu Lai, October, 1971.

The USO was (and still is) a great organization. They went out of their way to make the life of the soldier as tolerable as possible. The show in Chu Lai with Miss America was great. It was a big deal, and I was fortunate to be able to go. We laughed and sang. When Miss America and her lady friends came and mingled in the crowd, this grunt dreamed of home just a bit more! The USO did a lot of little things all the time to keep guys in good spirits. I still have the "Short Timers' Calendar" provided by the USO in Chu Lai. It was a picture of a grunt wearing a helmet and combat boots. He was real "short". The helmet was divided into segments, so the last 120 days of one's tour could be highlighted and marked off. I received my calendar after I moved out of the bush to Chu Lai. I colored in the days as they passed until I left country. The last 14 days were never colored in, indicating that I left country two weeks before my tour was to be over (I actually left 16 days early). I also modified my calendar, adding a couple of arms, some color, and a few "comments". I had plenty of time to doodle now that I was out of the bush.

My USO Shortimer's Calendar.

Typhoon Hester was not nearly as pleasant an experience as the USO show. Hester had winds in the neighborhood of 100 mph and made landfall just north of Chu Lai. I remember going out on the beach while the eye was passing over, then heading back in as the back side approached. The winds of the storm caused widespread destruction in Chu Lai. According to one report I read, three Americans and about 100 Vietnamese were killed by the storm. The storm damaged or destroyed 123 aircraft, and 75% of the structures on the Chu Lai base were damaged.

Aftermath of the typhoon Hester that hit Chu Lai in October, 1971.

Other than that, life was returning to a sense of normalcy. I did stand before the E5 board and passed that little test, receiving my E5 promotion after returning to the States.

More and more rumors began to swirl around about the 23rd Infantry Division (Americal) standing down and going home. As September turned into October, these rumors became more than rumors. October brought the definite news—the division was going home. The schedule for the stand downs for each of the units in the division was announced. There were many units that would be standing down from those in the field, the artillery batteries on the fire bases, and the support troops in the rear. The 4th/3rd would be standing down on October 15th, and ship dates (to home or other units) would be between October 18th and November 3rd; however, since I was in supply, I would be one of the last guys out—but that was ok. There was even some talk of me being part of the Division Colors escort out of the country. I wasn't too keen on that and was glad that idea got changed. Even though I would be behind a lot of others, I knew I was going home now… that was all that mattered… Larce was going home too, but Dale and Charlie didn't have enough time. They were moving on to another unit further north. Eventually they both made it home too!

The day finally arrived. It was November 5, 1971. I had spent six months with B-4/21 in Duc Pho and six months with D-4/3. I was 16 days shy of my full 12-month tour…. 349 days was long enough…. I was going home!

I had been moved from Chu Lai to Da Nang in preparation to fly out. I had to pee in the cup to be sure there were no drugs in my system before being scheduled for the Freedom Bird. (I had tried drugs one time back in Duc Pho and gotten violently sick, so I stayed away from them after that.) What a beautiful sight that Freedom Bird was! I remember well riding in the back of the duce-and-a-half to the tarmac. As we rounded the corner approaching the tarmac, there she was! A bright, silver bird shining in the sun! Everything else was OD or just dull, but not this bird. What a beauty! I remember the rise of emotion from deep within me as we approached. That emotion stayed capped until that beautiful bird was high above the sea and leveled off. Leaving Da Nang, she blasted out like a rocket, gaining altitude as fast as possible, all while turning toward the sea. After we leveled off, the pilot's voice came across the PA and announced we were out of Vietnam air space…. The entire plane erupted in cheers and cries! I didn't know another soul on that flight, but knew what each person felt at that moment. Though each of our emotional releases was unique because of the individual paths we had walked, nevertheless they were all still the same. WE WERE GOING HOME! WE HAD REALLY MADE IT!

We landed at McChord Air Force Base, in Washington State. We were then bussed over to Fort Lewis for processing, sometime during the wee hours of the morning. All I remember was that it was dark, damp, and cold—just like it had been when I was there on my way over to 'Nam. I guess some things never change…but "I" had changed, and these changes would become evident over time. I wasn't consciously aware of the changes that had taken place in me, but somehow I knew things were different. I was given the full complement of winter gear and told to turn in my jungle fatigues and boots. I stuffed my jungle fatigues and jungle boots into my newly acquired duffle bag and caught a cab to the airport. I had 30 days before having to report to Fort Hood, Texas. I was at Fort Lewis just a few short hours before heading to Florida, where Becki and Chuck were with her Mom, by way of Atlanta. During a layover in St. Louis, with the sun coming up there, I called Becki and told her I was on the way. What a moment! The distance was melting away. We talked and laughed and cried. She told me to hurry home. Nothing could slow me down! She called my folks in Atlanta, and they and my sister, Helen, met me during a layover there. Again, HOME! Even now I wipe a tear away as I remember the moment. The visit in Atlanta was short but good. My mind was already in Florida. Arrival there was sweet. There she was. What joy! And she was holding our boy who had been just two weeks old when I left. We all hugged in what was one of the best hugs of my life. I was home! I was back with my love! I was safe! We were safe! We were together! Becki had held back Chuck's first birthday party until my arrival. The sweetness of that moment, that day, that time, is a cherished memory! Vietnam was in my rearview mirror, fading away in the joy of the present.

We spent a couple of weeks in Florida with Becki's family before traveling back to Atlanta to spend time with my family. Then it was off to Texas and Fort Hood. We moved to Texas, found a little duplex for the three of us to rent, got settled in, and then I was off to report for duty. Larce Kyzar, his wife

Beverly, and their one-year-old daughter also lived in the area, and we spent some time with them. I was assigned to an armored unit and, on my first day, a group of us were assigned an Armored Personnel Carrier, or APC, to clean up. What? I spent a year in The 'Nam, and you want me to clean out an APC! I was a little mad about that, but that's the Army way. "It don't mean nothing!" Within just a few days of my reporting for duty, I was told the Army was offering early outs to Vietnam returnees. I said, "Sign me up!" In short order, I was processed out and became a civilian once again.

That was January 21, 1972. Uncle Sam had me for 19 months and five days—and my life was changed forever. Now, here I am, retired, some 44 years later and thankful to be here to tell my story. I have made it out of my tunnel—at least on most days. I returned to Atlanta and walked right back into the job I had with the phone company before I was drafted. It was like I had never left—only I had.

Slater Davis

THE AFTERMATH

There were adjustments to make returning to civilian life, especially since I was returning from a combat situation. Everyone who has been in combat has adjustments to make. I am convinced of that now, though I had no clue about this in 1972. I was not advised by the Army to be aware of the subtle, and not so subtle, changes I had experienced. I had already experienced the hurt of feeling rejected by my country because of the protests and demonstrations, but was not expecting this pain to affect me in any way as a civilian. I was never personally confronted by the anti-war and anti-military attitude that was prevalent in those days after I came home, but many Vietnam Veterans were. I learned from Larce, many years later, that when he applied for a job and the prospective employer learned he was a Vietnam Veteran, he was told he wasn't welcome there. They told him they didn't hire baby killers. Larce was not a baby killer. He had been a fine soldier and had served honorably. This really hurt Larce deeply and he carried this wound the rest of his life. It hurt me, too, when he told me about it. Recently, I was having a conversation with a young man who is serving proudly and professionally in the United States Air Force. He knew that I was a Vietnam Vet and because of that he told me, "Tell your buddies we all know about them. Every time someone thanks us for our service we know it's because of what each of you went through. We owe you guys so much. Thank you!" I wish Larce and Darrel could have heard that. I wish that every Vietnam Vet could hear that. Thankfully, today we have learned a hard lesson from

149

our experience back then. For me, in 1972, life was the same as before, but also very different. Things had changed. I had changed.

First, there were now three of us. When I first left home, there had only been two. This was a big adjustment. This new little guy had no clue who I was. That took some time too. Spending those short months in Texas was very difficult for us. Becki and Chuck had developed into a family while I had been gone, and I was intruding into that. If we had spent our first months together with other family back in Florida or Georgia, and been faced with this challenge, we might not have dealt with it. We might have run from it and gone our separate ways. In Texas, however, we were all alone; we were all we had. We had to work it out. I remember being really angry one day and just leaving the house. I don't remember what I was angry about, but I was. I had never been angry like that before. I stayed away several hours before returning home. I don't remember what all happened that day, but I guess we figured things out. We must have done it right, because we are still together 44 years later.

There were other adjustments that had to be made over the years. I spent a lot more time alone after returning from Vietnam. I could sit and be quiet for a long stretch. Noise, for me, was a real distraction at first. Sudden noises were an even greater distraction. Sometimes things would just happen, and there was nothing that could be done except to move on. One such time was July 4, 1972. We were sitting in front of our apartment in Atlanta with another couple and their small child, grilling burgers and enjoying an evening together. Then someone in the apartment complex shot off some fire crackers. I was on the ground and in the bushes for cover before anyone, myself included, knew what had happened. It was all sheer reaction that had been programmed into me for 19 months. I was totally embarrassed, our friends were confused, and Becki was scared. I shook it off and we finished our evening, but I was unsettled for a while after that. On another occasion, a couple of years later, Becki was standing beside our bed to wake me up. She reached out and touched me, and I came up out of the bed, threw her on the floor and landed on top of her before I realized where I was. Again, it was just a reaction to something that got triggered. I wasn't dreaming about Vietnam. I wasn't even thinking about Vietnam. I just reacted. My actions in both of these two examples (there were others) just happened out of the blue. The only explanation for me was Vietnam. We were both scared, but we dealt with it as best as we could. I apologized. We talked about it, not really knowing what to say or how to explain what had happened, and moved on. And...she still loves me, too. Then there was the guy at work, sometime in the late 1970s, who came up behind me and popped a paper bag as a practical joke. He doesn't know how close I came to popping. Even today, I still don't like unexpected loud noises. Go figure!

Over the years, as a family, we did a lot of camping for our family getaways. We enjoyed the out-of-doors and the family time. On several of these camping trips, though, while hiking with the family through the woods, I would find myself back in the bush. I don't think the family ever noticed this, but boy I did. I could feel the anxiety rising as I began to survey the woods that surrounded me. I had to get a grip and get my head in the right place. At first this was difficult, but over time I have learned to put the thoughts aside and enjoy the moment...the present. Today I love being in the woods and even enjoy long, solitary walks in the woods. If a thought of Vietnam comes to mind during these walks, I'm reminded to be thankful.

As time went by, life seemed to settle into a normal existence. I was prospering at work, now as a PBX installer. Our second son, Christopher Michael, was born in January, 1976. Later that same year, I finally heard the soft voice of God calling in my heart. I became a Christian that spring. Life was good. I was back in college, working toward a degree. But there was more to come.

I don't remember what triggered this, but sometime in the 1980s, in a moment of vulnerability and openness with Becki, I was remembering and talking. I made the passing comment that I had never gotten a parade like the WWII guys got. (As I look back on this moment, I can now see there was a lot of "stuff" that was bubbling up. I didn't recognize it at the time for what it was.) The following day when I returned home from work, every tree in our front yard had a yellow ribbon tied around it. There was a huge "Welcome Home" sign hanging from the front of the house. One of my brothers, John; my sister, Helen; my parents; and Becki and our two sons, Chuck and Chris, greeted me with hugs and welcome homes, thanking me and loving me. I was REALLY HOME! To this day, whenever I meet a Vietnam veteran, my first words are, "Welcome Home", for I have truly felt we never received that.

In 1987, our family took a camping trip to Washington, D.C. and then traveled down the Skyline Drive and The Blue Ridge Parkway back to Georgia. We spent a week in D.C., seeing many of the sights there. One of the sights we planned to see was The Wall (The Vietnam War Memorial containing the names of over 58,000 Americans killed in the war). The four of us made our way to the plaza where the Wall is located. It was a beautiful setting. We sat in the grass in front of The Wall, back away from The Wall itself, taking in the entire sight. How impressive that massive black wall was! I couldn't walk the path that ran in front of The Wall. I did not personally know anyone whose name was on The Wall. I felt unworthy to walk such a hallowed path. So we sat in the grass, the four of us, and I remember feeling so alone. I cried...just a tear, at first...then I began to weep. I'm not sure if I was weeping for those listed on the wall, the rest—who made it home, or just for the whole thing. Becki tried to console me, and both Chuck and Chris—who were 16 and 11 at the time—wrapped me in their hugs. I am sure they didn't understand what was going on. How could they, if I didn't even know, but they joined Becki in attempting to console me. I just kept my thoughts to myself. We sat for a while longer and then got up and moved on. It was still a beautiful day. I have since walked that path in front of that big, black wall; and even gotten an image of a name from the wall for a friend. It still is a hallowed place, in my mind; a reminder, again, of the cost of war, very real, very personal, very special.

Then there was 2003 and the invasion of Iraq by America and other nations. I found myself totally immersed in this action by watching the 24-hour news channels. I was quickly becoming obsessed and moving toward being a basket case. I wasn't sleeping much and found myself remembering stuff. It was a weird time. I began to give all of the feelings and emotions to the Lord, Whom I had come to know in 1976. HE helped me get my mind in the right place and settle my emotions. After that I got the idea that I needed to find my buddies. I think this was God's way of helping me really get out of my tunnel, or at least deal with it. I started going through some of my old stuff and found an address book from 'Nam with everybody's name and address. So I typed up a bunch of letters and mailed them. I also began searching the Internet for names I remembered. I had no idea what lay ahead! The first response I got was a day like no other! I opened my email, and there was an email from David Bruski, one of the squad leaders of 4th Platoon in Bravo Company. He had gotten my letter and responded to the email address I had included. I felt my emotions rising up as I clicked on it to read. Was he glad to hear from me? Would he not want to make contact? Would he even remember me? To my relief, he was excited that I had reached out to him. Wow!

I was ecstatic. I ran downstairs shouting, "I found Bruski. I found Bruski!" Becki gave me a big hug, and we talked about David and what he said in his email. I was on cloud nine. How many more would I hear from? This was going to be great! What would they be like? How would life be treating them? Hearing from Bruski motivated me all the more to pursue the men of 4th Platoon. It would only be a few days, however, before my cloud nine would turn into a tornado and my motivation disappear. I received a letter from the wife of Darrel Fuhs. Darrel had been my squad leader in 4th Platoon after Tim Frater moved to CP Platoon. She wrote that she had received my letter of inquiry about two months after Darrel had passed away. I wrote back expressing my sadness for her, but didn't dare tell her the despair that I felt when I learned of Darrel's death. I missed him by two months. For a time I went into a funk. I had been hit really hard by Darrel's death, and wasn't sure I wanted to go on with this search. Thankfully, Becki encouraged me to continue. After some time I got back into the search, knowing better what might lie ahead, and how to deal with the surprises—good and bad—that might come. I began getting responses from other former platoon mates. From these responses came more information leading to more of the men. I had sent a letter to the address I had for Gary Dolen (Gary had been our RTO) from my 1971 address book. The address was his parent's home, and they still lived there. At first, they all thought my letter was some type of solicitation based on the address label and typed return address, so they didn't give it much attention. Gary finally opened it, and discovered I was looking for him. When he contacted me he was able to give me information on two or three other men. One of those was Vince Varel. I had been searching for Vince using the Internet, but I had been spelling his name wrong. Gary straightened me out there, and I soon got a hit on his name on the Internet. Vince, an employee of the USDA, had written an article in a cattlemen's magazine on the effects of cattle urine in the stockyard. That was the only hit I got on Vince's name, so I contacted the publisher of the magazine with my story, and he passed my contact info along to Vince. This allowed him to contact me if he wanted, and within a few days I got an email from him. We still laugh about that article being the tool used to get reconnected.

There were other successes. For example, I found the brother of David Olender, and he was able to put the two of us together. Another success was finding Lonnie Johnson (Flash). The letter I had mailed to the address in my old address book was returned. I had begun searching the Internet for Lonnie Johnsons in Texas, for that was the place my address book showed as his home. According to my Internet search, there were a 'billion' Lonnie Johnsons in Texas. I began making phone calls to the ones who were listed to be about my age and marking names off the list. Finally, I located him! He lived in Duncanville, Texas, and was part owner of an art shop in Plano, Texas. I couldn't believe it! I had traveled to that area many times for work-related technical training, and we could have hooked up if I had only known. We decided we needed to get together, so we planned to meet at a midpoint, in Vicksburg, Mississippi. A short time later, Becki and I spent a weekend with Lonnie and Jan (Lonnie's wife) in Vicksburg, becoming friends all over again.

While searching the Internet, I came across some old stories about LZ Debbie and FSB San Juan Hill. One of these stories mentioned a Lt. Colonel Vernon Sones as the battalion commander of the 4th/21st in 1971. I thought this would have been Bravo Company's battalion commander, so I searched for him on the Internet. I got a hit and made a phone call. The result was an hour-long telephone conversation that began a wonderful relationship with Vernon and his wife, Helga. Vernon had quite a bit of information in his possession about Bravo Company (and the rest of the battalion) and volunteered to make copies and send them to me. This information was extremely helpful in finding the members of 4th Platoon from 1971. Later it would help others find men from the entire company from that same time frame. Becki and I had the pleasure to meet the Sones when we traveled to Washington, D.C. a few years later.

The search process continued throughout 2003. As we got in contact with each other, emails began flying back and forth between all the men. I had the pleasure of informing everyone when I made a new discovery, and more emails would fly. I also had the sad job of reporting disappointing news that I discovered. Many of the guys asked me if I had found any information on Paul Ashley, the man who had been injured on LZ Debbie by blooper shrapnel. I had not, but began a special effort to see what I could find. The results of this search proved to be a double-edged sword. I learned that Paul had made it home from 'Nam, but he had passed away in the year 2000. The reaction from the guys to this news was the same— "Good, he made it. I wish he was still here." By the end of 2003, I had found the status of 33 of the 36 men listed on the April 1971 4th platoon roster. Unfortunately, nine of the men had already passed away. Two of the men I located did not want to be reconnected. It was difficult for me to understand that at first, but I have come to realize that each of us has our own experience and must walk it.

My searches finally ended in 2006 when I learned that Doc, Eli Williams, had passed away. It took quite some time to be confident that Eli was, in fact, our medic. No one could remember his name. He was known as Doc to all of us. Vernon Sones had sent me an April, 1971, company roster, and platoon assignments were included. Medics, however, were not assigned to a platoon on the roster. All of the medics were assigned to Headquarters and were "loaned" to the field companies. All of Bravo company's medics were listed on the Bravo Company roster, but were not listed by the platoon they served with. I shared all of the medic's names from the roster with the rest of the guys, and no one was positive. Some thought Eli was the right one, but they weren't sure. I finally was able to make contact with one of the medics on the list, and he confirmed that Eli was with 4th Platoon. Then I learned that he had already passed away and was buried in a National Cemetery in New Mexico. In a telephone conversation with an employee at the cemetery, I learned that Eli had a brother, and I asked if they could contact the brother on my behalf. They said they would, so I wrote a letter about 4th Platoon and Eli being our medic. I mailed it to the person at the cemetery in hopes of contacting Eli's family. I never heard back from anyone.

As the emails flew back and forth in 2003, everyone began sharing pictures with each other. Ken Sciford's wife, Cathy, set up a website and started collecting the pictures, posting them for everyone to see. Then there was talk of a reunion. In the spring of 2004, fourteen of us—along with the wives and girlfriends—had our first reunion. It was in Las Vegas. I'll never forget registering at the front desk of the hotel. As I was standing at the front desk waiting while my check-in was being processed, I noticed a man stepping up next to me and being helped by another person at the front desk. I acknowledged him with a nod, and he did the same to me. As I looked back toward the person who was handling my registration, the man who had just arrived spoke to the hotel employee helping him. I hadn't recognized him, but the voice was unmistakable. It was Tim Frater. Both of our registrations were delayed for a few minutes as we cheerfully greeted each other. We have had several reunions over the years since. Each one has been special in its own way, but the first one was really unique. It was a big step for all of us. None of us knew what to expect going in. We all came with a little trepidation about what might happen. Becki told me later, that the wives were the same way. The gathering was a great success. In addition to our private rooms, we had all chipped in to rent a suite to use for a gathering place. In just a matter of minutes after we began gathering, all anxiety disappeared in a rush of laughter, hugs, and a few tears. Stories were told. Pictures were looked at. Memories were clarified. Friendships were reestablished. Becki told me later that the wives were amazed at how their husbands had all of a sudden become so talkative. It was like we had become 19- and 20-year-olds all over again, laughing and telling stories, remembering things.

Our first reunion in Las Vegas
standing L to R Jack Beaupre, Charlie Sauer, Lonnie Johnson, Gary Dolen, David Myers, Slater Davis, Ken Sciford, Dale Doege, David Olender. Kneeling in front L to R, Tim Frater, Tom Duran, Ken Cameron, Vince Varel and Dale Hill

Over time the email traffic has continued, but today, at a slower pace. Unfortunately, some more of our members have passed away. A few years ago, a new website was set up to better organize the pictures to tell the story of 4th Platoon. This site is found at http://bbb4thplatoon1971.webnode.com .

The story of 4th Platoon is being viewed several hundred times each month by folks from all over the world.

We were a bunch of young guys who hadn't figured life out. Most of us were draftees. And—really—we didn't have much in common with each other. If we had not served in 'Nam together, we probably wouldn't know each other today, much less be interested in each other. But we <u>did</u> serve in 'Nam together, and that changed everything. We bonded in some way that I can't explain. It was special. I still can't tell you the names of the guys I served with in Delta 4/3, but every one of the guys in 4th Platoon, Bravo Company, 4th/21st are special to me...and always will be. I don't try to figure it out. I just enjoy them and have great respect for them.

COMING TO FAITH

My Vietnam experience contributed to who I am today. Many other experiences have also helped shape me. My childhood and family life were big shapers in my life, but there is one experience that did more than shape me. This experience changed me completely...it was coming to know God in a personal way. I had a great childhood, growing up in a wonderful family. Life was good. Every Friday night was family night at our house until we became teenagers. Family night meant games, s'mores, laughter, songs, and just a good time. We didn't have a lot, but as a child I was not aware of missing anything. I was loved, along with my two brothers and one sister. After supper most every night we had family devotions. I learned how to pray and many of the stories of the Bible at the family table. My Dad was a Presbyterian minister. Mom was a stay-at-home Mom until we were all in school, and then she began teaching in high school. In the 1960s, as integration was happening, Mom volunteered to be a teacher in the all-black high school in Griffin, our home town. As an adult, I consider my parents as heroes. It took becoming an adult to realize that though.

We were in church whenever the doors were open. I can remember as a child having my little pins all hooked together on my coat, displaying my long history of perfect attendance in Sunday School. When I was 12 years old, I was of the age that kids in our church attended what was called Communicants' Class. In this class we learned basic church doctrine, studied the Catechism, and then were tested on what we learned. I passed with flying colors and was allowed to officially join the church as a Christian. I was a leader in the youth group and sang in the choir. I even served on a couple of church committees representing the youth's point of view.

As I grew into my teen years, I began to lose interest in church and the things that went on there. This became a source of conflict between me and my Dad. By the time I was 16, I was a true rebel. I was causing my family a lot of pain and sorrow. Dad confronted me one time and told me I was breaking my Mom's heart. I blew this off. It was all about me.

This attitude continued through the completion of high school and into college. During the summer after my first year of college, I met Becki. She too was a rebel, so we had a lot in common. Our relationship deepened and we planned to marry at the end of my second year of college—May, 1969. In the spring of that year, my parents gave us a trip to a conference in Gatlinburg, Tennessee, called Faith at Work. My sister, Helen, and her new husband, Dan, also attended. This was a life-changing weekend for Becki and me. Becki gave her heart to God, becoming a Christian, and I thought I did too after this emotional weekend. I realized I had caused a lot of pain in my family, and when we came home I apologized to Mom and Dad for all of that. Things were good. Life went on. We were married May 30, 1969. Dad married us.

I got my job with the phone company in Atlanta and we moved from Griffin to Atlanta. We joined a church there and were actively involved. Being in church took care of Sundays, but had no effect on the rest of the week for me. My life was just as full of rebelliousness and selfishness as it had been when I was a teenager; it just showed itself in different ways. Then came Vietnam and the aftermath.

In 1976, after we had bought our first home and had our second child, Chris, things began to change. We had been attending church regularly for a couple of years (that's what you're supposed to do, right?), and I began hearing things I had heard all my life, but I was "really" hearing them for the first time. In addition to being reminded of God's great love for me, I was also confronted with God's holiness and justice. The idea that God must punish sin was something I am sure I had heard before, but it hit me as a fresh, new thought. I can't remember ever hearing it quite like I was hearing it at this time. I knew that Jesus had died for the sins of the world (one of those answers I learned when I was 12), but I never really understood why Jesus died for the sins of the world. I learned it was because someone had to! God's justice required it. I had claimed to be a Christian since my emotional experience in Gatlinburg in 1969. My life, however, had never changed except to apologize to my parents...and that just seemed the right thing to do at the time...and I was trying to be a good person if it didn't interfere with things too much. Now I was being gently confronted with the reality of my inability to live up to God's standard and the cost of that—my rebelliousness, my selfishness, my attitudes, my attempts to be "good", my thoughts and actions, all fell far short of God's perfect standard. The Bible says, "All have sinned (that included me) and fall short of God's glory." I learned that is really what sin is, missing God's mark. I now knew I faced the wrath and justice of God because of it. God is perfect. I knew that. But I had never connected that He could not let this very imperfect guy into heaven. Now I was learning if He did let me into heaven without dealing with my imperfections (sin), heaven would no longer be heaven! A payment had to be made. I had to pay! The Bible says, "...the wages of sin is death...". I had earned that wage! His justice demanded a payment. However, we have this in the Bible also— "God so loved the world He sent His only Son..." That's one verse most people in America are probably familiar with—John 3:16. His justice demanded a payment. That was the 'why' Jesus had died for the sins of the world. Jesus paid what God's justice demanded. But Jesus was also perfect. He had not "fallen short of God's glory". He did not deserve the justice He received. He willingly took that punishment for me. I was broken in my heart by this tremendous show of God's love for me. It was no longer the world that Jesus died for...it was me! I was given something I surely didn't deserve. That is grace! It was in the spring of 1976 that these truths came to my heart, and I surrendered. I gave up control of my life to God. I repented. That means I turned away from all 'my stuff' and turned to His stuff. I accepted God's payment for my sin (His Son, Jesus) and in response gave Him my life. I let Him have control. I was no more the long-lived rebel that I had been. I was forgiven. I was really a Christian. I belonged to Him now.

Since then God has led my life through many challenges and changes. Sometimes I went willingly, even eagerly; other times

I fought against it until I was once again gently brought back to the reality of His great love for me, and the reality that His way is best. Did God wipe away all my memories and thoughts of Vietnam? No, He didn't. But God has taught me over the years He can be trusted even when I don't understand something, and there is a lot I don't understand about Vietnam and its impact on me. When those thoughts arise in me I let Him and Scripture guide me. He has taught me that no matter what may happen, or may have happened, He can use it to bring about good in the lives of those who love Him and follow Him. Reading the Bible has become something I enjoy. I had read it before, but never really understood it. Now it made sense…but more than that, the words of Scripture now teach and direct me. I have heard it said that the Bible is God's "love letter" to His children. I guess before I became a Christian I was reading someone else's mail! No wonder it had not been clear to me. His way is truly best…and the only way to eternal life.

The Bible records Jesus saying in John 14:6, "I am the way, and the truth, and the life; no one comes to the Father but through Me." (NASB) In the spring of 1976 I had finally seen that He was the Way. He is where forgiveness is found, and where eternal life is. He is eternal life. If you are reading this and have never seen this truth, I would invite you to consider it. May I suggest grabbing a Bible and begin reading in the Gospel of John. He is to be found by those who look for Him. He brings with Him forgiveness and eternal life to all who surrender to Him.

EPILOGUE

My tour in Vietnam changed me. I have said my tour was much easier than what a lot of guys experienced, and that is true. A big reason for that is the hard work that was done and the sacrifices that were made by many before my tour began. I was one of the replacements for men who had been killed, or seriously wounded, just before my arrival. I've learned their names, and had the honor to meet one of them at a Bravo Company reunion in 2013. I never personally knew someone who was killed in Vietnam, and this contributed to a feeling of not having done my share. A platoon of Charlie Company in our battalion, working the same area we worked, hit a large booby trap; seven men were killed, and 13 others wounded. It could have been our platoon. It wasn't. I cannot explain why I made it home unscathed and others did not. Sometimes I have felt guilty about that. I don't think anyone can explain these types of things. I am now thankful for not being exposed to so many things that others were. I am thankful for the leaders of Bravo Company, especially 4th Platoon, who watched out for us; and I am thankful for the men I served with as we helped each other and protected each other in a treacherous time in our lives. Today I am thankful to be able to tell this story. Easy is a relative term. My tour was not easy for me.

I have accepted the fact that what is written on these pages is part of who I am. Some people talk about healing and closure. I'm not sure I know what that means. I now seek to embrace my life experiences, especially those that have shaped me. I cannot change what happened. It happened. It IS the past, but it still happened. And it contributed to who I am. It is not who I am, but it is a part of me...and it always will be. <u>It belongs</u>. I can no longer deny that. I am now proud that I served, though once I was not. I was embarrassed and ashamed, having felt the rejection of my nation. But no more! I was young, but I <u>was</u> a soldier. I was a grunt who served in Vietnam.

"Welcome Home!"

Slater Davis

4th Platoon, Bravo Co, 4/21, 11th LIB, Americal; 1970-1971

1st Platoon, Delta Co, 4/3, 198th LIB, Americal; 1971

CPSIA information can be obtained
at www.ICGtesting.com
Printed in the USA
LVHW01s2123110917
548046LV00001B/6/P